Souvenirs from Japan

Souvenirs from Japan

Japanese photography at the turn of the century

Margarita Winkel

with a preface by Prof. Willem R. van Gulik

Bamboo Publishing Ltd - London

Colophon

First published 1991 by
Bamboo Publishing Ltd
719 Fulham Road, London SW6 5UL
in association with
Ukiyo-e Books bv
Langebrug 34
2311 TM Leiden
The Netherlands

Text copyright © Margarita Winkel 1991
Preface copyright © Willem van Gulik 1991
Photographic material copyright © Ukiyo-e
Books bv 1991

ISBN 1-870076-18-4 cloth
ISBN 1-870076-58-3 paperback

A catalogue (CIP) record for this book is available from the British Library.

Designed by Robert Schaap, Bergeyk,
The Netherlands
Printed by Drukkerij De Kempen, Hapert,
The Netherlands

Cover illustrations

front
Women Greeting. Women bowing to each other in gesture of greeting. The use of compositional techniques such as the careful scattering of straw in the foreground and the arrangement of props may indicate that this piece was by von Stillfried.

back
View of Mount Fuji from Kashiwabara

Foreword

In December 1989 the Schilling collection of nineteenth-century Japanese photography was acquired by the Dutch bookstore Ukiyo-e Books in Leiden from Lempertz Auction house in Cologne, Germany.

When I initially viewed these works with the owners, we were all struck by their exceptional quality, both in the pristine condition and in the diverse imagery. Almost immediately the idea of a publication was born.

During my survey of the existing literature in Western language sources dealing with Japanese tourist photography of the late nineteenth century, I was convinced of the need to devote time on what appeared to be a relatively undocumented area. Earlier writers had concentrated only on well-known Western photographers, Felice Beato and Baron von Stillfried, who worked in Japan a number of years. Little attention was paid to the indigenous industry of tourist photography which flourished from c. 1880. It has only been in the last decade that serious interest in the field increased among Japanese scholars.

In this book it has been my aim to integrate both Japanese and Western sources and to address some of the relevant questions which have been left unanswered in Western literature. My own training as an anthropologist explains the emphasis of the text on the socio-cultural meaning of the Schilling photographs, although their artistic and historic value no doubt warrants further indepth treatment by art historians and historians alike. Following a brief introduction concerning the provenance of the Schilling collection, I have attempted to outline the cultural and historical setting within which Japanese photography developed in the second half of the nineteenth century. Then I focus upon photography as a technique and as a profession; a description of the early days of photography in Japan serves as an introduction to various aspects of Japanese souvenir photography, the latter being particularly germane to the collection presented in this publication.

I would like to thank Christer von der Burg and my husband Chris Uhlenbeck for having the good sense to buy and thereby reunite the Schilling collection. The advise and information given by Mr. Herman Moeshart was greatly appreciated as was that of Professor Willem van Gulik who critically read an earlier draft and Ms. Cleo Whittaker has thoroughly corrected the first English version.

My greatest debt lies with Amy Newland whose expert knowledge of Japanese art and history, combined with her meticulous editing qualities has lifted this publication in content and form to a level which I would never have been able to attain by myself.

Margarita Winkel
Leiden, June 1991

Contents

Editorial note

*Japanese names appear in Japanese order,
with the family name written first.
Where the names of Japanese rivers, bridges
and temples, etc., are not commonly known in
the West nor have entered into English usage,
the full Japanese name is given, i.e., the name
and the geographical appellation such as the
river, Tamagawa.
For those Japanese words which have entered
into English usage diacritical marks have also
been omitted, as in the case of the city of
Tokyo.
Numbers within brackets in the running text
correspond to the caption entries.*

Preface

In his eighteenth-century treatise on Western-style painting the *seiyō gadan,* the Japanese scholar and painter Shiba Kōkan (1747-1818) stated, "One realistically drawn picture is worth ten-thousand words...", which accurately expresses the supremacy of the visual image over any description in words. To depict figures and images as realistically as possible was the ideal sought after by men like Kōkan, who belonged to the Edo-period (1600-1868) group of artists and scholars called *rangakusha* (Scholars of Dutch Learning). These scholars were eager to study and to apply the teachings of modern Western science and technology to a number of fields. In art, the influence of 'Dutch learning' was to emphasize the technological rather than the artistic interpretation of Western pictorial art. The assimilation of Western art techniques in traditional painting styles led to novel ways of realistic representation. And so the Dutch, who were the only Westerners permitted to stay in Japan during its period of National Seclusion from 1639-1853, played an important role in the country's transition from a medieval to early modern society. This included the transformation from a speculative to a rationalistic approach to Western science and technology.

It is, therefore, not surprising that one of the first daguerreotype cameras introduced to Japan came in through the Dutch trading post Dejima located in the Nagasaki Bay around the middle of the nineteenth century. Shortly thereafter, the physician and physicist of the trading post Jan Karel van den Broek (1814-1865) was offering instruction in photography and writing the first manuals for the Japanese on the use of the camera and photographic techniques. Due to van den Broek's efforts, his successor, Julius Pompe van Meerdervoort (1829-1908), although himself not very knowledgeable about the photographic process, was able to continue experimenting with photography together with some of van den Broek's pupils. Among Pompe van Meerdervoort's own pupils were Ueno Hikoma and Uchida Kuichi, two pioneers of Japanese photography who are treated in this book.

The introduction of photography and modern printing methods to Japan in the nineteenth-century precipitated the decline in popularity of *ukiyo-e* woodblock prints that had hitherto served as the medium in which visual information was transmitted. Nevertheless photography was influenced by the more traditional medium. The themes already known from woodblock prints were also taken up in photography for example, and the artisans who had formerly worked with colour printing-blocks were now applying their skills in the careful addition of colours to albumen photographs. Both *ukiyo-e* and photography also served as souvenirs of the vivid images of traditional Japan. Yet, while the former were intended to represent the fleeting and transient, the latter, as seen in pieces in the Schilling collection, were tangible reminders of the visual world of late nineteenth-century Japan, which no historical record can ever adequately describe.
As a result, these photographs while speaking their own very special and select language, are clear and understandable to all.

Willem van Gulik
Chairman, Society for Japanese Arts
Chairman, Netherlands-Japan Association

The Schilling family at their residence in Tokyo.

The Schilling Collection of 19th-century Japanese Photography

This book presents a selection of 179 photographs drawn from a collection of 510 amassed at the turn of the century by the German forest engineer Schilling during his stay in Japan. All the photographs in the Schilling collection are printed on albumen paper and their quality is excellent, free of any fading or browning, which is explained by the fact that they were simply laid in albums with linen or silk-embroidered covers. This is different from most photographic albums of this period in which the photographs were pasted into albums of cardboard paper and therefore particularly prone to acid staining and discolouration.

Little information concerning Herr Schilling's travel to and life in Japan is available. However, based on the proceedings of the Mitteilungen der Deutschen Gesellschaft für Natur- und Völkerkunde Ostasiens ('German Proceedings of the Society for East Asian Nature and Ethnology') in Tokyo, it can be conjectured that Schilling arrived in Japan in the autumn of 1899. On November 29 he entered the society as a lifelong member (he is listed as R. Schilling) and apparently came to Japan as a temporary advisor to the Ministry of Imperial Affairs concerning the management of the imperial forest resources in Japan.

Schilling's collection was accompanied by a lacquer-covered family picture album of "Herr Königlicher Preussischer Regierungs- und Forstrat R. Schilling" ('R. Schilling, Civil Servant and Forest Advisor to the Royal Prussian Government'). Assembled in 1905/6, it contains over 200 small snapshots which documented Schilling's voyage to Japan, his travels

there, his return trip via California and his first years back in Germany. It provides a valuable source for reconstructing Schilling's life in Japan. Based on the photographs in the album, Schilling appears to have had a permanent residence in Tokyo. Snapshots labelled 'the first residence' ('Erstes Wohnhaus'), depict a relatively modest two-storied wooden house which was located in Aoyama in the Akasaka district. Included also are illustrations of the heavily moustached Schilling himself, being served tea or posing in a kimono. Schilling eventually moved to a much grander Western-style wooden house in Aoyama, which was surrounded by extensive grounds. Photographs in the album show other equally impressive Western-style homes also in the neighbourhood.

During his sejourn in Japan, Schilling was accompanied by a woman who was described in the album as *Tante* ('aunt') and by a couple of dachshunds. It can also be deduced from these photographs that as part of his assignment Schilling travelled throughout Japan, visiting such places as the scenic Kiso mountains in Nagano prefecture and the Northern island of Hokkaido, where he visited Ainu communities.

The last record of his activities in Japan seems to have been a lecture which he gave for the Society on February 4, 1903, entitled *Die Besiedlung von Kronland auf Hokkaido* ('The Colonization of the Crown Lands in Hokkaido'). By September of 1903 Schilling was back in Germany and living in Berlin at Leipzigerplatz 7. Not long afterwards, he assumed a position in Hinternah in Thüringen. The last pictures in the album are of the Oberförsterei in Hinternah.

The Rokumeikan, a famous example of Meiji architecture. It was designed by the British architect Josiah Conder and was meant as a meeting place for upper-class Japanese and foreigners.
Courtesy Rijksdienst Beeldende Kunst, The Hague

The setting: Nineteenth-century Japan

Tokugawa Society

On July 8, 1853, the American naval squadron under Commodore Matthew Calbraith Perry (1794-1858) entered Edo (now Tokyo) Bay and anchored at Uraga. These were the first foreign ships to land there for over two centuries. Perry delivered a letter from the American president to the Tokugawa shogunate demanding the opening of Japan's borders to Western trade. His arrival precipitated the end of Japan's long period of seclusion which had begun in 1639 when the shogunate forbade contact with the outside world. The events leading up to this decree had unfolded a century earlier, in 1543, with the arrival of the first Europeans in Japan, the Portuguese. They established trade relations with the country and in 1549, the first Portuguese Jesuit missionary, Francis Xavier (1506-1552), came to Japan to spread the Christian faith. The proselytizing efforts of Western and Japanese Christians were so successful that their activities were viewed as a threat to the political stability of the country, as well as a menace to Buddhist temples. Religious persecutions began in the late sixteenth century and in the early seventeenth century the first anti-Christian edicts were issued. Christians were sought out and forced to apostasize, otherwise face death. In 1639, in an effort to remove the threat of Christianity and Western intrusion, the shogunate instigated a policy of National Seclusion *(sakoku)* and the country closed its doors. Westerners were prohibited free entry, Christianity was banned and the Japanese were not permitted to leave. The only regular contacts with the outside world were through the Chinese and Dutch trade missions in Nagasaki, located on the southernmost island of Kyushu, and the Koreans, trade with whom was restricted to the island of Tsushima.

The Tokugawa shogunate (Bakufu), who were responsible for the policy of *sakoku*, had begun their rule in 1600 and remained in control until 1868, fifteen years after Perry's arrival. The over 250 years of Tokugawa rule were characterized by relative internal peace. Following years of internal strife, the Tokugawa family, under the lead of Ieyasu, reunified the country and in 1603 received the title of 'Shogun' from the emperor. While sanctioned by the imperial house, actual political power rested with the shogunate. The main threat to the shogun's position came from the fissionary tendencies of the socio-political structure: the shogun had allotted fiefs to daimyo, who were his sworn vassals. These fiefs were basically autonomous political units, with their own bureaucratic and judicial apparatus, and the lords or their vassals were authorised to collect taxes within their own territory. As a means to keep the daimyo in check, the Bakufu imposed a system of alternate attendance *(sankin kōtai)* which stated that the daimyo spend half of the year in their fiefdoms, while their families were forced to live as 'hostages' in the vicinity of the shogunal castle in Edo. Furthermore, the shogun controlled all access to the emperor who, with the court nobility, were confined to the imperial palace in Kyoto. Thus the emperor could not be used for secessionary ambitions of the more powerful daimyo.

Tokugawa society was principally divided into four hereditary social groups in a system known as the *shi-nō-kō-shi*, which was based on the twelfth-century moralistic Neo-Confucian theories of Chu Hsi. The highest was the warrior class (*shi*, or samurai), to which the shogun and military elite belonged. They controlled the administration of the country. Next were the farmers (nōnin), followed by the artisans (kōnin). The merchants (shōnin) were at the bottom of the scale; together the artisans and merchants, who tended to reside in urban areas, are generally known as the townspeople (chōnin). According to Neo-Confucianist theory, merchants were unproductive members of society as they handled commercial affairs, which accounts for their low social rating. But their inferior social position was not in line with their actual cultural, financial and intellectual contribution to society, and in the course of the Tokugawa or Edo period this gap widened.

With the establishment of the shogunal headquarters in Edo, the city became the political and bureaucratic centre of Japan. The requirement that the daimyo families maintain a residence in the city created great demand for goods and services. Sectors of the chōnin catering to this group became exceedingly wealthy. In contrast, the costs imposed upon the daimyo put a strain on their economic resources, and during the Edo period many lower-ranking samurai families became impoverished and forced into activities considered below their status. Through marriage with those of the merchant class, for example, some samurai exchanged their higher social rank for financial security. Others chose to abandon their warrior status even without such liaisons. Apart from financial rewards, giving up their hereditary status would enable them to participate freely in the exciting and bustling life of the city.

Edo is estimated to have been the largest city in the world in 1700, with more than a million inhabitants. Within this enormous urban centre, the chōnin population created their bourgeois society, an extremely sophisticated world of transient pleasure and entertainment: the ukiyo ('floating world'). The Bakufu, concerned to avert too flamboyant a display of wealth by merchants, passed sumptuary laws which imposed severe restrictions on housing and clothing of the townspeople. For example, chōnin were not allowed to wear silk as this was a privilege of the samurai. Since conspicious consumption was

risky, townspeople preferred to spend their money on entertainment and on refined objects. In this climate, the pleasure quarters, such as the Yoshiwara in Edo and the Shimabara in Kyoto, flourished (nos. 6, 18-19, 40, 115-116). For men who were not samurai, pleasure-seeking was a politically innocent pursuit that presented a chance to escape from the rigid social system. Within their own world the chōnin were autonomous and status was determined by entirely different criteria: a good reputation could be earned by being knowledgeable about the latest fashions, by being witty, and by being reputed as a great lover. To be held in high esteem as the demimonde of the city, you had to be a full-fledged participator in the entertainment world and be entertaining yourself. This atmosphere of the ukiyo was illustrated in the popular fiction of such writers as Ihara Saikaku (1642-1693) and Santō Kyōden (1761-1816).

Japan had had a long history of adoption and assimilation of foreign political and cultural elements, as exemplified by the country's relationship with China early in its history. Even during the period of National Seclusion, knowledge about the West trickled in via books and Nagasaki residents, although this was carefully controlled. Yet, with the arrival of Commodore Perry, opinion differed greatly as to whether renewed contact with the outside world was desirable. Some daimyo were very much in favour of ending Japan's isolation, convinced of the technological and military superiority of the West and that ending the period of seclusion was Japan's only escape from backwardness. These daimyo supported the advancement of Western science in their country by sending able men in their entourage to pursue rangaku ('Dutch Learning'), a term used to broadly designate Western learning. This support for Western learning by daimyo also greatly facilitated the early introduction of photography. Without the sponsorship of men like Toda Tadayuki (1810-1884), who could afford the expensive photographic equipment, it would have been impossible for such pioneers in photography as Ueno Hikoma and Horie Kuwajirō to buy and experiment with the latest model wet-plate camera. Shimazu Nariakira (1809-1858), daimyo of

Satsuma, seems to have used photography to try to pursuade his hesitant countrymen of the necessity to turn to the West and end Japan's isolation.[1] But leading families opposing any intrusion whatsoever were also numerous and powerful. Finally, the end to isolation did not come about through a consensus within Japan, but through external pressure from what were indeed superior military powers. The United States pressed for a trade treaty, which was concluded in 1854, and soon treaties were signed with the Netherlands, Great Britain and Russia, eventually opening the ports of Shimoda and Hakodate (1854), Yokohama and Nagasaki (1859) and Kobe (1868) to foreign trade (nos. 123-124, 157-159). During this period the Bakufu was caught in a dilemma. They did not want to provoke Western nations and therefore strove for a degree of national consensus regarding the opening of the country. On the other hand, Western nations demanded more and more concessions and the Bakufu tried to delay the finalizing of trade treaties for as long as possible. This resulted in a situation of mounting internal strife. It took the Japanese some fourteen years to resolve the dilemma and this period is known as the Bakumatsu–'the *fin de siècle* of shogunate government'.

The Meiji period

In 1867, the last shogun, Tokugawa Yoshinobu (1837-1913), resigned his office and in 1868 the 'Restoration' of imperial rule was proclaimed. Within a year, the emperor and the new government moved from Kyoto to Edo. Edo was renamed Tokyo ('Eastern Capital'). The emperor, Mitsuhito (1852-1912), who initially resisted the intrusion of the West, now became one of its foremost supporters and acted as a guide to his people on the road to Westernization. This period was named Meiji ('Enlightened Rule').

Although the Western trade agreements with the Bakufu were considered unfair and humiliating by the Japanese, the Meiji leaders nonetheless felt the need to be treated on an equal footing by Western powers and to be considered a civilized nation. Civilization meant Westernization: 'A wealthy country and a strong army' and 'catch up and outrun' were the political slogans of the day. By the 1870s the process of modernization, *bunmei kaika* ('Civilization and Enlightenment'), was in full swing. The Japanese vigorously adapted to Western practices, altering their social and legal rules, their personal attire, and the whole outlook of their country.

In Tokugawa society certain positions were the hereditary prerogative of specific families, and this applied to warrior, farmer, artisan and merchant families alike. Particular privileges had been allotted to them by the Bakufu, and in return the family provided a person suitable to fulfil the duty assigned. In 1869, however, the division of society into four classes and the hereditary family prerogatives connected with the fulfilment of specific duties were abandoned. Likewise, in attire, marks formerly denoting social status disappeared. The right of samurai to wear swords was abolished in 1876. Married women were discouraged from shaving their eyebrows and blackening their teeth, a custom denoting conjugal status. The empress stopped blackening her teeth in 1873, and the ladies of the court followed her example. The last group to give up this age-old habit were the peasant women in remote areas of the country[2] (no. 26). To many, this social levelling was very confusing, and they felt at a loss now that former social distinctions had so suddenly and severely been uprooted.

One of the most visible symbols of the drive towards Westernization was the construction of the Rokumeikan, ('The Deer-Cry Pavilion'), a huge establishment meant as a meeting place for foreigners and upper-class Japanese. The initiative to build the Rokumeikan came from the Meiji government. The aim was to promote social relations at an informal level between Japanese and foreigners, to which the name refers as it is an allusion to a Chinese poem dealing with social intercourse between persons of different nationalities. In spite of this intention the scale tipped to the Western side: it was designed by the British architect Josiah Conder (1852-1920), who had been hired by the Meiji government to teach architecture, and who came to Japan in 1877. As was characteristic of his buildings, the Rokumeikan was a hotch-potch of European, Moorish and even American Victorian building styles. It was opened in 1883 and contained a ballroom, a dining-room under the supervision of a French chef, and a billiard lounge. English cigarettes, German beer and American cocktails could be bought there and all visitors were expected to appear in Western dress. Married couples were invited jointly to parties and banquets, indeed a novelty for the Japanese. The Rokumeikan, which was severely damaged in 1893, came to be strongly associated with the excessive adherence of Meiji politicians to Western customs. Its name was subsequently used to denote the years during which the adulation of the West was at its peak. The turning point of the Rokumeikan era came in 1889, at a masked ball given by Prime Minister Itō Hirobumi (1841-1909). This event, and more specifically the behaviour of the Japanese politicians present, became a source of scorn and ridicule in the Japanese press.[3]

Meanwhile Westernization had an enormous impact on the outlook of the country. Changes in attire were not restricted to those elements that designated social status. Hairstyle was the easiest and cheapest to alter. The emperor, in his function as a trendsetter, had his top-knot cut off in 1873. Men quickly took to Western hairstyles and by 1890 the top-knot had become a rare sight: 'If you tap a shaven and top-knotted head you will hear the sound of retrogression, but if you tap a close-cropped head of hair you will hear the sound of civilization and enlightenment', ran a contemporary song.[4] The adoption of Western-style clothing was a much more elaborate process. For men, the outcome was at first a hybrid, a very common mixture being a Western hat worn in combination with a traditional kimono. The reason why hats and umbrellas were among the first items to be adopted was that they were not expensive, cost being the most serious inhibition in the process of changing to Western costume. Moreover, Japanese clothes were better suited for the country's hot summer climate.

Japanese women took longer to change over to Western dress. For a while, women dressed in foreign garb were jeered at by men who themselves wore Western clothing. The empress appeared in public in a Western-style robe for the first time in 1886, recommending that Japanese women follow her example. But, as the cost of doing so was very high, only women from rich families could afford to. One of the main problems was the manufacture of the clothes. For centuries Japanese women had sewn their own and their families' garments. Contrary to the simple design of the kimono, Western dresses were complicated and required a totally different way of sewing. In 1887 the empress issued a proclamation advising the adoption of Western sewing methods in the making of Western-style clothes. However, she recommended the use of domestic materials, so that local manufacturing techniques could be improved.

Women also lagged behind in adopting new hairstyles. Here again, initial steps towards Westernization were met with fierce criticism. In newspapers and magazines new haircuts for women were depicted as absurd and unbecoming. In 1872 a decree forbidding women to cut their hair was issued, but in 1885 a movement promoting Western haircuts for women was established. It was argued that the traditional hairstyle was inconvenient and it was alleged that the oil applied to stiffen the hair was unhygienic. From the 1890s onward Western hairstyles for women became more common.

Initially starting with the treaty ports, towns experienced a rapid increase of Western-style barbershops and tailors, food-stores and butchers. New products like bread, matches and crushed ice were sold. Artisans had a hard time adapting to the manufacture of Western-style clothes, umbrellas, leather shoes and household furnishings. They had to learn to produce entirely new devices like watches, lamps and rickshaws. But the ones who have carried the heaviest burden in accomplishing Japan's industrial revolution were probably young unmarried female laborers from poor rural areas. They had to work in coal mines and textile factories under the most dreadful conditions.[5]

Early Meiji dress. The first items of Western-style clothing to be adopted by the Japanese were the hat and the umbrella.

It was not only personal attire and the outlook of cities that were affected. Once railways and telegraph poles made their way into the country, even in remote areas, life was not as it had been. Some of these new practices required the alteration of deeply rooted taboos. Despite centuries of Buddhist prohibitions on eating meat, this suddenly became acceptable, even desirable, as all sorts of positive effects were thought to result from meat consumption. Here again, the emperor set an example, but it is reported that he did not care for meat, nor for any other foreign food, with the exception of wine.[6]

Until the Meiji Restoration the emperor and empress were a highly respected, but shadowy couple, but now they came to the forefront, leading their people through new and unfamiliar territory. The emperor frequently appeared in public throughout the country, attending the opening ceremonies of many Western-style buildings, and in 1872 he inaugurated the first railway line from Tokyo to Yokohama. The distribution of the imperial couple's portrait had formerly been restricted, but in 1872 the photographer Uchida Kuichi (1844-1875) was given the honour of portraying the emperor and empress. These photographs became immensely popular and were used as the basis for paintings by Takahashi Yuichi (1828-1894) and Goseda Hōryū (1827-1892) and woodblock prints designed by Utagawa Kunisada IV (1848-1920), Toyohara Chikanobu (1838-1912) and Toyohara Kunichika (1835-1900).

Photography was to symbolize the new, modern and enlightened society of Meiji Japan, and it was taken up by the Japanese with alacrity. Its rapid spread is illustrated by *shashin shihei* ('photo-money'), which was brought into circulation in 1869. Each note of currency was printed with a photograph as a means of preventing forgery, while at the same time serving as a token of the new era. The improvement in and general availability of photographic techniques, however, made forgery a simple matter in just a few years and the use of 'photo-money' was soon abandoned.[7]

Two prints from the series **Mirror of Imperial Eminency, (Kōkoku kiken kan),** *1889, by Toyohara Chikanobu.*
Two of the many 'imperial family' prints published in the Meiji period. These were obviously designed after photographs of the imperial family which were widely circulated at that time.

The image of Japan in the West

Japan witnessed a rapid influx of Western culture, but the adoption was not a one-sided process. Although Japan may not have forced a new world-view upon the nineteenth- century Victorian, it definitely exercised a great influence on British, American and French literature and the arts. The general public, vaguely conscious of the existence of a country named Japan, was now seized by a fad for things Japanese. This interest in Japan internationally was particulary influenced by several events. One of them was the discovery in 1856 by the French etcher Félix Bracquemond (1833-1914) of a volume of sketches (*manga*) designed by the Japanese woodblock artist Katsushika Hokusai (1760-1849). This event set the stage for the maturation of the Japonisme movement in the 1860s, when Japanese art poured into France as part of the country's infatuation with exotic culture. With Bracquemond's find, the work of *ukiyo-e* artists like Hokusai would have a profound impact on French art. The nineteenth-century French Impressionists admired the *ukiyo-e* artists' treatment of contemporary subjects, an aim they were also striving for. Both were 'movements that freed the artist's imagination and glorified his mundane subjects'.[8] Yet, the influence of *ukiyo-e* extended beyond the mere copying of motifs; the affinity that the Impressionists felt to have in common with the Japanese *ukiyo-e* artists on their outlook on life and art is reflected in statements like Duret's, 'the Japanese are the first and finest Impressionists'.[9] Exhibitions, such as the 1867 Paris Exhibition Universelle also played an important role in introducing Japanese culture to the public.

Another event had a huge impact in America and resulted from the visit of a Japanese mission there in 1860 to ratify the trade treaty concluded by Commodore Perry. The members of the mission took part in American parades and festivities, which attracted crowds of spectators, and which generated an interest in Japan. And finally, the English International Exhibition of 1862 in London triggered off the British craze for things Japanese, whether it be art objects, bric-a-brac or the 'Jolly Jap', a type appearing on stage as an unusual touch to variety shows and musicals. The ambiguous image of Japan appealed to the exotic needs of the Victorians: 'an eastern country which was curiously civilized but hardly European, a nation of beautiful and refined but also enticing and "improper" women, a land which needed the benefits of civilization through trade and yet one which had a splendid culture to confer upon the west'.[10] 'Things Japanese' were an exotic source of inspiration for poets, prose-writers and dramatists, and several hundreds of travel books on Japan were published. Travelling to Japan was very much in vogue.

Information about Japan for the interested Westerner was provided through the seemingly endless stream of travelogues, novels and discourses on Japan. Two of the most influential writers were the French author Pierre Loti (1850-1923; born Julien Marie Viaud) and the American Lafcadio Hearn (1850-1904). Loti was the first European writer of literary importance to visit Japan. His most popular novel, *Madame Chrysanthème*, was first published in the French newspaper *Le Figaro*, and then in 1887 as a book. The novel is autobiographical and describes his impressions of Japan as a French naval officer and of his temporary 'wife', *Madame Chrysanthème*. This work initiated a new genre in late Romantic literature which revolves around an exotic setting, as here where a Western man is intimately involved with a Japanese woman, only to desert her upon the inevitable return to his own land. Giacomo Puccini's opera *Madame Butterfly*, which is modelled on Loti's novel but tells the story from the woman's point of view, pictures the 'devoted and tragic oriental woman faithfully waiting with cherry blossoms and lanterns for her heartless western lover'.[11] The outcome of these 'desertion novels' is not always desertion, like in the very popular book *My Japanese Wife* by Clive Holland, first published in London in 1895. Here the hero does not leave his temporary wife but returns to England with her. Whatever the final outcome of the romance, however, Japanese women were invariably described as doll-like creatures, little playthings, maybe ugly, but droll and amusing.[12] The opinion on Japanese men is more negative, although not all are as harsh as Loti:

[about women]- *pretty little physiognomies, little narrow eyes peeping between slit lids like those of a new-born kitten, fat pale little cheeks, round, puffed-out, half-opened lips. They are pretty nevertheless, these little Niponese, in their smiles and childishness. The men, on the other hand, wear many a pot hat, pompously added to the long national robe, and giving thereby a finishing touch to their cheerful ugliness, resembling nothing so much as dancing monkeys.[13]*

Loti's picture of Japan 'was to hold all but complete sway over the popular mind until Lafcadio Hearn enlarged it [the image] and softened its harshness'.[14] But again, Hearn views Japanese women as very different creatures:

For it has well been said that the most wonderful aesthetic products of Japan are not its ivories, nor its bronzes, nor its porcelains, nor its swords, nor any of its marvels in metal or lacquer- but its women. ... How frequently has it been asserted that, as a moral being, the Japanese woman does not seem to belong to the same race as the Japanese man! ... -the Japanese woman as prepared and perfected by the old-time education for that strange society in which the charm of her moral being, -her delicacy, her supreme unselfishness, her child-like piety and trust, her exquisite tactful perception of all ways and means to make happiness about her,-can be comprehended and valued.[15]

Apparently, Prime Minister Itō had keenly sensed this prevalent attitude. The German Ottmar von Mohl, who had served as the adviser to the Meiji court, had suggested that the Japanese should adhere to wearing the national costume at court receptions, as was the custom at several European courts. But Itō asserted that European dress was now most fitting, as, contrary to Europe, Japan had only just left the Middle Ages behind, and he suggested that the Japanese would probably be able to return to their native costume at court receptions in later centuries. He is reported to have remarked that Japanese women wearing kimono would be considered as hollow festival dolls by the Westerners present.[16]

Great differences exist between Loti and Hearn. Loti, a casual visitor to Japan, was primarily concerned with the exotic and sensational, and unrestricted by moral inhibitions. Hearn was a more profound and systematic observer. He organized his subject around specific themes, like history, religion, and folk-tales. Yet, both were convinced that Japan is basically incomprehensible to the Westerner. Loti stressed that 'we have absolutely nothing in common with this people'.[17] Hearn, despite his more scientific approach, his marriage to a Japanese, his long stay in Japan and the fact that he finally became a naturalized Japanese citizen, saw Japan as a dream:

Yes-for no little time these fairy-folk can give you all the soft bliss of sleep. But sooner or later, if you dwell long with them, your contentment will prove to have much in common with the happiness of dreams..... Really you are happy because you have entered bodily into Fairyland,- into a world that is not, and never could be your own.[18]

Hearn published many books stressing the value of Japanese

native culture and was very disappointed at the end of his life when he saw his new countrymen increasingly embracing Western attitudes.

Westerners in Japan

The foreigners who visited Japan came with different attitudes, had diverging goals and were at variance in their opinions on the country. At first their movement was restricted to the limited zones around the treaty ports. Entry into the hinterland was permitted only to those who held a special licence. Exceptions were made for railway and other technical experts who were needed in remote areas. A handful of teachers, much in demand, settled in places previously untouched by foreign influence.

Until the 1880s most of these foreigners had a clear mission: conducting business, spreading Western technology or the gospel, or documenting the country. One famous exception was Isabella Bird, who managed to obtain a travel permit as early as 1878 and wandered through the remotest parts of the country. Most treaty port residents never went beyond the 24-mile limit, and did not even care to, being satisfied with 'the contents of the mail-bags, social events and a perfection of their physical comfort', as an American visiting the treaty ports in the 1890s commented.[19]

There were those who hated Japan and those who venerated it, the latter sometimes carrying their adoration so far that they became more Japanese than the Japanese, like Lafcadio Hearn or Ernest Fenollosa (1853-1908). Fenollosa strongly advocated the rejection of the growing Western influence on traditional Japanese art forms, which he considered superior.

The real tourists, visiting Japan just for fun, came in the 1880s, when travel restrictions were eased. Tourists arrived in increasing numbers. There were the globe-trotters, the professional travellers, who stayed in Japan for varying lengths of time. As Japonisme was in full swing abroad, many came searching for the picturesque life that they encountered in prints, photographs and teacups, a life which by their very presence Westerners helped to destroy. In Yokohama, 'Curio Street', the central avenue in the city's Japanese sector, was the place to go for lacquer, cloisonné, bronze sculptures and porcelain. These products were mostly made for the export market (nos. 15, 158). Curio-hunting could be pursued in many other places as well. Osman Edwards in his *Residential Rhymes,* published in Tokyo in 1900, jibed at the globe-trotters and curio hunters:

Doodle san *will leave Japan*
With several tons of cargo;
Folk will stare, when all his ware
Is poured into Chicago.

There's silk, cut velvet, old brocade
And everything, that's "jōtō",
And ancient bronzes, newly made
For dealers in Kyoto.[20]

Advertisements in travel-guides for shops in Tokyo, Kyoto, and the treaty ports were abundant. Loti provides us with a vivid description of the actual buying procedure:

The chief occupation in this Japanese country seems to be a perpetual hunt after curios. We sit down on the mattings, in the antique-sellers' little booths, take a cup of tea with the salesmen, and rummage with our own hands in the cupboards and chests, where many a fantastic piece of old rubbish is huddled away. The bargaining, much discussed, is laughingly carried on for several days, as though we were trying to play off some excellent little practical joke upon each other.[21]

The 1888 *Guide to the Japanese Islands* classified trips according to the traveller's state of health and pioneering spirit. The well trodden tracks were for 'delicate persons and those who dislike accommodations at Japanese inns'. The next category consisted of more daring explorations, for those who loved 'the curious and the picturesque' and were in 'robust health'. Those who wanted to keep well away from the beaten track could venture on still more exotic expeditions.[22] One thing loathed by foreign visitors were the insects that nestled in the bedding. The absence of 'proper' beds was another source of annoyance, as was the lack of privacy. Endless staring by the locals wore on the nerves of the travellers, as well as frequent loud disturbances during the night. Then there were the mixed public baths which were abhorred by foreign visitors. However, the largest obstacle to a pleasant stay was Japanese food. Opinions were quite unanimous: Japanese food was horrible. Nonetheless, many loved Japan for the beauty of its countryside, for its temples, shrines and cities and for its lovable, alluring population.

As a rule, Westerners were disdainful about Japanese attempts to take up occidental ways and appearances. They came in search of the Japanese fairy-tale and were shocked at what they considered to be an artificial mimicry: so unbecoming to a people who had such a beautiful native style! 'We thought it a piece of barbarism to discard the easy, graceful kimono for the stiff, ill-fitting European costume' complained Katherine Baxter in her book, *In Bamboo Lands,* which was published in New York in 1895.[23]

The photographs visitors took home betrayed their conservative tastes. The romantic sights and scenery, enjoyed for centuries by the Japanese themselves, became the places also favoured by the tourists, and were a popular subject in their photo-albums. As concerns the depiction of Japanese people, however, the foreigners preferred scenes conveying Japan's exotic and feudal image. These photographs were mostly produced in studios using painted back-drops and consisted of nostalgic images of days gone by. This type of photograph came to be known in Japan as *Yokohama shashin* ('Yokohama photographs'), after the name of the port where many photographers producing this type of work were settled.

The Chief Interpreter to the Perry Expedition and his Assistant. A lithograph by T. Sinclair, made from an Eliphalet Brown jr. daguerreotype. This lithograph was used as an illustation in the 1856 journal documenting Perry's voyage.

Early photographic techniques and their introduction to Japan

In contrast to other Western technology, only a few years elapsed between the invention of photography in Europe and its introduction to Japan. The Japanese named this new device *shashin*, literally meaning 'reproducing reality'. Although the adaptation of this new process occurred relatively quickly, it was not without flaws.

The daguerreotype

After Louis Daguerre (1787-1851) developed the first widely applicable photographic process, the daguerreotype, the French government acquired the patent on the technique and gave 'the world of science and art' this invention as a present in 1839. In this process a silver-plate, which had been polished with pumice stone, was put into a box containing iodine crystals to make it photosensitive. While still in the dark the plate was then inserted into a holder and both were placed in a camera. Exposure time varied from ten minutes to three-quarters of an hour, which made posing a tiresome affair. The photograph was developed in a box containing heated mercury and the result was finally fixed with salt. The whole procedure was time-consuming and extremely expensive, resulting in just one photograph which could be easily damaged. Moreover, the daguerreotype reverses the image like a reflection in a mirror.

The first daguerreotype camera was introduced to Japan in 1848. It was ordered by Ueno Shunnojō (1790-1851), a Naga-saki merchant, who sold the camera to Shimazu Nariakira, the afore-mentioned daimyo of Satsuma.[24] At this early stage it was the daimyo with a special interest in Western science who encouraged and financed photographic experimentation. Those who practised photography were men who were often sent by their feudal lords to Nagasaki to be trained in 'Dutch learning'. Such an education was the only way Japanese could acquire knowledge of Western scientific developments during the Edo period. Three Dutch medical doctors who were successively stationed at Dejima played a key role in the dissemination of early photographic technique. The first and foremost was Jan Karel van de Broek (1814-1865), followed by Julius Lydius Catharinus Pompe van Meerdervoort (1829-1908) and Antonius Franciscus Bauduin (1820-1885).[25] The earliest extant photograph taken by a Japanese is a daguerreotype portrait of Shimazu Nariakira, and it dates from 1857.

A few years earlier, in 1853, the daguerreotypist Eliphalet Brown Jr. arrived in Japan as a member of Commodore Perry's fleet. According to the report of the expedition, he took 400 to 500 photographs in the different ports visited by the fleet. Some of these photographic images were used to make lithographs, which were subsequently used as illustrations in *A Journal of the Perry Expedition to Japan 1853-1854* by Samuel Wells Williams, published in 1856. Due to the mirror-effect of the daguerreotype process, Brown had to take precautionary measures: in order for the photograph to come out 'right', samurai had to reverse the overlap of their kimonos and wear their swords on the wrong side. As this precaution was not always taken, some of the later lithographs, which were based on the photographs, show the attire of the samurai reversed. Unfortunately, the print shop which had published the Perry report was destroyed in a fire in 1856, and all but three of Brown's original daguerreotypes were lost.[26]

Wet-plate photography

The daguerreotype was succeeded by the wet-collodion process which was developed by the British sculptor and photographer Frederick Scott Archer. Archer first described the process in 1851 in an article in the British journal *The Chemist*. Glass-plates covered with a thin film of wet collodion,[27] were sensitized in a silver nitrate solution and immediately inserted into a camera. These plates had to be exposed and developed while still wet, as collodion becomes less photosensitive when it dries. In contrast to the daguerreotype-plate, the collodion-plate, once exposed and developed, functioned as a negative from which more than one positive print could be obtained. Exposure time was much shorter, a few seconds being sufficient. Despite its advantages, photography using wet collodion was still a tremendous undertaking. The time pressure was great and the photographer who chose to work outside of a studio had to have his darkroom, the necessary chemicals and lots of fresh water immediately at hand. The equipment was enormous and very heavy.

The collodion process was introduced to Japan between 1854 and 1859. Again, foreigners were responsible for disseminating the new technique from the three treaty ports: Nagasaki on the southern island of Kyushu, Yokohama near Tokyo and Hakodate on the northern island of Hokkaido. In Nagasaki Pompe van Meerdervoort trained several Japanese including Uchida Kuichi and Maeda Genzō. After 1854, the Dutch ceased to be the exclusive disseminators of Western knowledge, and in the Nagasaki area a French photographer named Roche imparted knowledge of the wet-collodion technique to the Japanese. In Yokohama Shimooka Renjō was initiated in the collodion photographic process by an otherwise unknown American visitor named Winshin. The most famous photographer from the north of Japan, Kizu Kōkichi, became acquainted with the wet-plate procedure through the first Russian consul in Japan Goshikevitch, whom he met in Hakodate.[28] Eventually, the knowledge of photographic technique was no longer confined to those who had contact with foreigners. The first

two Japanese professional photographers, Shimooka Renjō, and Ueno Hikoma in Nagasaki, for example, trained a substantial number of new photographers. Nevertheless, the three treaty ports remained the centres of photography. Foreigners in these cities also provided an important means of support for the growing numbers of professional photographers. In 1870 there were already over a hundred professional photographers and by 1877, there were that many in the Tokyo area alone.[29] And, with the introduction of the collodion process, Japanese photography prospered. The necessary materials were cheaper and easier to obtain, an important consideration in Japan in those days. Earlier, pioneers experimenting with photography had sometimes gone to great lengths to obtain ingredients. Ueno Hikoma had tried to procure ammonia by putting meat into stone jars and leaving it to decompose at the back of his house. But the unbearable stench that it produced occasioned complaints from his neighbours, who took the matter to court and Ueno was forced to move.[30]

Prints were first made on paper covered with collodion, but this was superseded by albumen (egg white) paper, which was introduced to Japan in the early 1870s. It soon became very popular; all the photographs in this book were printed on albumen paper.

The dry-plate process

The first commercial production of dry-plate photography was in 1874 by the Liverpool Dry Plate Company. Like the wet-collodion process, dry-plate photography also employs glass plates, but gelatin and silver bromide, rather than collodion, is used to sensitize the plates. The necessity for speed which had made the wet-plate process such a hazardous undertaking was alleviated and dry-plates could be obtained ready-made and kept until they were needed. The process was introduced to Japan in 1883. While the dry-plate process greatly facilitated the development of photography in Japan, thus causing an increase in photo-studios, it nonetheless co-existed

Blind Masseur. *Blind masseurs typically carried a flute and cane. They would walk through the streets whistling in order to make customers aware of their presence. The distinctive use of a cameo to frame the subject and the identifying number to the right of the figure suggests that this photograph may be by Felice Beato.*

with the dry-plate process until the turn of the century.

As photographic technology became easier and the number of photo-studios grew, the photographer turned from scientist to shop-keeper. This change was reflected in the terminology: pioneer photographers were called *shashin-shi* (*shashin*, 'photography'; *shi*, 'masters'). Later, photographers and their workplaces were termed *shashin-ya* ('photography shops').

Pioneers of Photography in Japan

Initially in Japan, as elsewhere in the world, superstitions about cameras and photographs were widespread. 'Once photographed your shadow will fade, twice photographed your life will shorten', was one way in which the Japanese expressed their distrust of this new apparatus. Vampire-like qualities were also ascribed to photography: 'sucking out your lifeblood, it shortens your lifespan'.[31] But suspicions gradually decreased. In 1871, reporting on a visit to the Asakusa temple in Kyoto, Baron Hübner notes the photographs for sale in the tiny shops along the road leading to the temple: 'The Japanese are past masters in this art, which has taken root here within the space of a few years and is practiced today in localities as yet unseen by any European'.[32] In *Madame Chrysanthème*, Loti describes how upon his arrival in Nagasaki, the ship was invaded by boat-loads of vendors who, among other things, sold 'quaint photographs'.[33] And although these might have been photos specifically aimed at foreign tourists, the Japanese themselves had grown less wary of the technique. Loti is amused by Chrysanthème's collection of portraits depicting her friends, 'their photographs stuck on visiting cards, which are printed on the back with the name of Uyeno, the fashionable photographer in Nagasaki'.[34] The Japanese took up photography in the same way they adopted other Western innovations.

Pierre Loti, Madame Chrysanthème and their friend Yves, one day set out for the shop of 'the best photographer in Nagasaki' to have their photograph taken:

There are, in Japan, photographers in the style of our own, with this one difference, that they are Japanese, and inhabit Japanese houses... His [Ueno Hikoma] signboard, written in several languages, is stuck up against a wall on the edge of the little torrent which, rushing down from the green mountain above, is crossed by many a curved bridge of old granite and lined on either side by light bamboos or oleanders in full bloom. It is astonishing and puzzling to find a photographer perched there, in the very heart of old Japan.[35]

Ueno Hikoma and Shimooka Renjō, the first two professional Japanese photographers, both set up their business in 1862. Both encountered many difficulties at the outset, but eventually became very successful. Loti remarks that when they arrived at Ueno's studio it was crowded with people—including high-class Japanese women—waiting to have their photograph taken. Of Shimooka's business it is said that his clients arrived before his gates opened and were still there after sunset.[36] Many of their customers were foreigners.

Ueno Hikoma, 'the acknowledged master of portrait photography in mid-nineteenth-century Japan'[37] was born in 1838 in Nagasaki. As mentioned above his father, Ueno Shunnojō, a merchant who had access to the Dutch trading mission at Dejima, was the first Japanese to obtain a camera. After studying Chinese classics at a school in Hida, in Ōita prefecture, Ueno Hikoma returned to Nagasaki where he learned Dutch and studied with Pompe van Meerdervoort. There he met Horie Kuwajirō (1831-1866), with whom he conducted many photographic experiments. In 1862 they collaborated on a three-volume book on Western science and the Dutch language; the third volume contained an essay on collodion photography, the first publication in Japanese on the subject. Ueno established his first studio in 1862 in his back garden, but his debut as a professional photographer was not straightforward. Since the special foreign trading privileges of the Ueno family had been withdrawn following the opening up of the country, the family income had been reduced to a very modest level. Photography was still considered a highly suspect activity by the Japanese and initially most of his clients were foreign residents. Gradually, the Japanese dropped their attitude towards photography and from 1865 they came to the studio more frequently. Amongst the customers were many of the activists who were involved in the upheaval of the Bakumatsu period. These samurai had their photographs taken by Ueno as a keepsake for their families in case they were assassinated. This was not an altogether unrealistic anticipation as indeed several men such as Nakaoka Shintarō were murdered within a year of being photographed. Ueno's prices are known to have been very high: 'a single portrait cost the equivalent of a craftsman's monthly earnings. It was double for two people, and foreigners were charged twice that sum'.[38] Ueno did not restrict himself to the studio, nor did he confine himself to the well-to-do. He also photographed panoramas and many scenes depicting ordinary life in contemporary Japan. He died in 1904.

Shimooka Renjō was born in 1823 in Shimoda, Izu province (now part of Shizuoka prefecture). Shimoda was one of the first treaty ports to be opened to the Americans, with the first American Consul, Townsend Harris arriving there in 1856. Shimooka went to Edo to study painting, but after seeing a photograph for the first time he became totally enamoured with the process. Shimooka was not a scientist and had a hard time mastering the photographic technique. Through an interpreter he learned the general principles of photography from Harris, although unfortunately not the essentials. In 1859 he moved to Yokohama where he apparently obtained photographic equipment through an American, Winshin, who was leaving the country. Yet, with his limited knowledge, Shimooka was unable to use the equipment properly.
It was not until 1861 that he actually produced a photograph and he subsequently became a successful and famous photographer. Around 1875, Shimooka moved to Asakusa in Tokyo and thereafter concentrated more and more on his painting, leaving his son in charge of the photography business. He had grown tired of the fierce competition between the ever increasing numbers of photographers.[39] He died in 1914.

The Venetian Felice Beato (1825-1904) went to Malta in 1850, where he set up himself as a photographer. Beato and James Robertson, an English colleague in Malta, went from there to Constantinople, and in 1855 they were appointed to photograph the Crimean War. They first achieved fame with an exhibition in London of these photographs. Thereafter Beato became a British citizen, and with Robertson, he went to the Near East and then to India. In India Beato again proved himself as a competent war photo-journalist. His images of the British reprisals at Lucknow, in 1858, for example, were the first to show corpses. In 1860 he met Charles Wirgman (1832-1891), a sketch-artist and correspondent for *The Illustrated London News*, as they accompanied the advance of the French and British armies towards Peking. A year later Wirgman travelled to Japan and once there, advised his friend Beato to follow him. Beato arrived in 1863 and together they established a photo-studio in Yokohama. According to a letter from Wirgman dated 26 September, 1863, in *The Illustrated London News*, they could not complain about lack of interest. Their house seemed constantly to be filled with Japanese officers 'who come to see my sketches and my companion Signor Beato's photographs. They are extremely polite and bring presents of fruit, paper, and fans'.[40] According to Edel, the main aim of their business was 'the commercialization in the West of that great novelty, *Japonisme*, the craze for all things Japanese'.[41] Wirgman and Beato also founded the first English-language Japanese magazine, *Japan Punch* (later *The Far East*).

In Japan, Beato again portrayed some sensational scenes, like crucified and decapitated Japanese criminals, and the corpses of Europeans slain by hostile Japanese. Accompanying the British Minister Parkes on a diplomatic visit in 1867, Beato managed to take a picture of Tokugawa Yoshinobu. However, he was not allowed to sell the photograph. Beato, nevertheless, produced many beautiful photographs of the country and people of

Japan: landscapes, towns, artisans, farmers and other aspects of what was still largely *terra incognita.*

Great damage was done to Beato and Wirgman's collection of photographs and negatives in the fire that ravaged Yokohama in 1866. Their studio burned down, but by 1868 it was clear they were back in business. At this time Beato published two photography albums: *Photographic Views of Japan with Historical and Descriptive Notes, Compiled from Authentic Sources,* and *Personal Observations During a Residence of Several Years,* commonly known as the *Views of Japan,* and *Native Types.* Beato and Wirgman ended their partnership in 1869. Wirgman was to concentrate on painting, sketching and journalism. He would play an influential role in introducing Western-style painting techniques to several important Japanese painters and printmakers. Beato continued his photographic business until 1877 when he sold out to the firm of an Austrian, Baron von Stillfried. Beato stayed in Yokohama as a general merchant until 1884 after which time he settled in Rangoon, Burma, where he established himself as an antique dealer, and where he died in 1904.[42]

Baron Raimund von Stillfried und Ratenitz was born in Bohemia in 1839. Like Beato, he travelled extensively before arriving in Japan, and he had served in the army of Austrian Emperor Maximillian in Mexico. He came to Japan in 1870, apparently for the second time, with the 'Imperial Austrian Expedition'. Von Stillfried decided to stay and established himself as a photographer in Yokohama. His photographs of Japan, shown at the 1873 Japan Exhibition in Vienna, brought him fame not only in Austria but also in Japan. He regularly changed the name of his firm; for example: Stillfried & Co. (1871-1874); The Japan Photographic Association (1876); and Stillfried and Andersen (1876-1879), the firm that took over Beato's stock in 1877. Von Stillfried and Andersen produced an album, *Views and Costumes of Japan,* in the late 1870s. Von Stillfried also worked as an instructor at the State Press, and he seems to have left the country in 1885.[43] He died in Vienna in 1911.

Among Western scholars there is some discrepancy over the precise take-over of von Stillfried's studio. Some claim that Kusakabe Kimbei, a supposed student of von Stillfried, acquired his stock and Banta elaborates by stating that von Stillfried's studio was assumed by Kimbei in 1885, and his stock passed on to Farsari in 1886.[44] Yet Robinson is of the opinion that von Stillfried, from his stock, 'sold a handsome portion to his former assistant, Kusakabe Kimbei, and the rest to A. Farsari'.[45] Handy says that Kimbei was 'assumed to have been active in von Stillfried's studio as apprentice, camera operator, or associate'. He acquired most of the stock and Farsari got 'the remainder'.[46]

The Schilling collection contains a substantial number of photographs documenting the devastations of the Aiki earthquake of 1891.

Souvenir photography

Despite the differences in scholarly opinion, however, over the acquisition of von Stillfried's stock, Farsari, Kimbei and Tamamura Kōzaburō were the most important photographers engaged in the production of souvenir photographs during this period. Not much is known about the life and background of A. Farsari. His name first appears in 1878, in *The Japan Directory,* the annual English business guide, as the manager of the Yokohama Cigar Company. In 1879 he owns a newspaper agency and in 1881 takes over the Stillfried and Andersen business, which marks the start of his photography enterprise. According to Worswick, it was: 'the most prolific of all commercial photographic firms in Japan'.[47] His firm produced tourist albums which were renowned for their exquisitely coloured photographs. Japanese sources unanimously concur that Farsari took over von Stillfried's stock. Evidence for this is seen on one of Farsari's labels, which states: 'A. Farsari en co. late Stillfried and Andersen'. On this label is reproduced the gold medal certificate as proof of the prize the Stillfried and Andersen firm had won in the 1883-4 Calcutta International Exhibition. Farsari appears to have remained in business until 1917.[48]

Japanese sources consider Kimbei (he used his personal name as his trading name) to have been a pupil of Beato, and not of von Stillfried. Kimbei (1841-1934)was born to a merchant family. In 1859 he arrived in Yokohama and, according to Japanese sources, he was employed by Beato as a tinter of photographs until 1863. Thereafter Beato taught him the tricks of the trade. In 1881 Kimbei established himself as an independent photographer, and at his height he had twenty people working for him, producing and selling photographic albums. He closed down his shop in 1914, and dedicated himself entirely to Japanese-style painting.[49]

Tamamura Kōzaburō was born in Edo in 1856. At the age of thirteen he became an apprentice to a Tokyo photographer and seven years later established himself independently in Asakusa, Tokyo. In 1882 he moved to Yokohama, where he remained in business until 1916 (no. 123). For some time, he and Farsari were partners. Tamamura is perhaps best known for his receipt of an enormous order in 1896 from a Boston dealer who wanted a million portraits depicting customs and famous places of Japan.[50]

K. TAMAMURA
The leading photographer of Japan,
is the place for tourists to get
THE FINEST PHOTOGRAPHS
in native costume.
(The finest collection of views,
the finest colored views)
The largest collection, the largest studio, the best artists,
and better than all, THE LOWEST PRICES.
- - - - - - - - - - - - - - - -
LACQUER COVERED ALBUMS
CHERRY LACQUER FRAMES
in great variety.
The celebrated artist *S. Shosaku* (known as the "long-haired Artist") is in my employ.
An inspection of my work is respectfully solicited.[51]

Photographs from Schilling's personal album, depicting Tante ('aunt'),
the woman who accompanied him on his voyage to Japan.
As a souvenir, these snapshots in a 'Japanese' setting were very popular
among foreigners. Tante is depicted in a kimono and in a rickshaw,
together with the driver employed by them.

Distinctive characteristics of Japanese tourist-photography were the choice of topics, the colouring of the photographs and the albums in which they were collected. Souvenir photography was at its peak during the last decade of the nineteenth century. Not only short-term visitors, but also foreign residents, were interested in the 'typical Japanese' photographs as a keepsake, or as a present to family or friends. Westerners who had never been to Japan and who were not able to afford such a costly voyage wanted to have photographic representations. Hence, large quantities of these photographs were ordered by foreign firms and exported to America and Europe at an increased pace. Exports peaked in 1897 and 1900, when 24,923 and 20,242 photos were sent abroad, respectively (exports officially registered by the Japan Trade Bureau). During this time most photographs were sent to the United States, while ten years earlier England and Hong Kong were the main destinations. The bulk was produced in Yokohama with a few exported photographs coming from Kobe or Nagasaki. Photography had become big business. The times when a photographer struggled to survive using his backyard as a studio had long gone. Farsari's listing in the 1881 *The Japan Directory* shows the potential of a successful photographic enterprise: he employed a manager, a clerk and five operators (photographers and their assistants), a printer with two assistants, a compositor, a bookbinder, a painter with sixteen assistants and two 'boys', and a carpenter - thirty-three people in all.[52]

Subject-matter

What was depicted in souvenir photographs? Foreign residents in Japan could go to one of the many photo-studios to have their portraits taken dressed up in a kimono, or sitting in a rickshaw, for example. Much cheaper were pictures made in the numerous *shajō*, rudimentary studios that were set up in the street, simply by hanging a backdrop. Here 'foreigners or Japanese could spontaneously decide to have a photograph made'.[53] When visiting a locality, like Kamakura, photographers were always present and made portraits of the visitors posing in front of the famous statue of the Great Buddha there.

Apart from personal portraits, the subject-matter of tourist-photographs can be broadly divided into three categories: customs and types; women; and famous views and places. Albums generally contained examples of each, although half to two-thirds of the imagery were from the third category.

Photographs depicting traditional scenes showed different aspects of 'typical' Japanese life. The choice of subject conformed to the Western stereotype of Japan: drinking tea, smoking, bathing and eating (nos. 11-12, 25, 43, 45, 80, 87); the customary bow in greeting (front cover); young women playing traditional musical instruments and games, or performing domestic tasks (10, 42, 44); samurai in full armour (14); various professions and handicrafts (8-9, 32-39); rural life (1-3, 27-31); street vendors (53-56); and wandering priests (46, 49-50). Some of these photos, particularly the ones which centre on outdoor events like processions and festivals, are more or less authentic depictions of contemporary Japanese life (17, 66-69). However, many of the images of Japan produced for foreigners were pure kitsch, barely concealed studio set-ups with actors ill at ease in their roles. Nevertheless, they are beautifully composed, executed and coloured. Westerners were interested in subjects that were commonplace to Japanese and Dower remarks that, were it not for Western interest, many occupations and the lower-classes would not have been photographed.[54]

The women portrayed in these albums are mainly lovely young girls dressed in beautiful kimonos, conveying a serene atmosphere in which the face of the girl is clearly the most important aspect. As Iwasaki remarks, Japanese women were for Westerners one of the main factors in the 'lure of the Orient'.[55] However, individual portraits (nos. 88-91) were not specifically produced for foreigners. It became a fad in Meiji Japan to have your own portrait made and miniaturised. They were used as calling cards or exchanged as keepsakes among friends. Furthermore, photographs of famous geisha were sold for the same reasons as depictions of famous actors: admirers wanted an image of their favourite idol.[56] Other photographs, however, were clearly meant to suit the foreign taste. The extensive use of 'real Japanese' props and the elaborate display of kimonos and hairdoes gives them an artificial feel (nos. 84-87). A line in blatantly pornographic photographs, for which girls of the poverty-stricken rural areas were recruited, apparently flourished at this time.[57] However, these do not seem to have been included in tourist collections.

Photographs of famous views and places included images of renowned buildings and sites such as traditional temples and shrines (nos. 126-130, 132-133, 137-138) as well as new Meiji buildings (112-114, 117-118, 149-150). Images of bridges (139, 146, 148); city-streets (111-113, 117-118, 160); and rivers and bays (136, 166, 168) were also an important part of this genre. Although seemingly contradictory, one characteristic feature of photographs of 'famous views and places' is the way in which humans are placed in the surroundings. Of course, scenes without the inclusion of people were a principal part of the genre, but images in which human figures played a significant role in the composition were also popular. A particularly common compositional arrangement was the placement of figures and/or objects in a scene set against a splendid, panoramic view (nos. 107-108). This approach is not unique to photography, as the same device is also used in woodblock prints. However, what is novel to these photographs is the combination of people and sites, seen, for example, in the pictures taken at Nikko and Miyajima (nos. 134, 137), where men serve to indicate the size of natural or man-made elements such as giant trees, revolving lanterns or huge *torii*. In both examples, the human presence is deliberate, an aspect not dissimilar from the carefully planned human actors in studio photographs. However, photography introduces yet another distinctive element: the depiction of famous places which are always crowded, like well-known resort areas; important bridges; or a popular theatre (nos. 119-120, 122, 154). In such photographs the presence of spectators is an integral part of the image. While their presence is not always deliberate, they are nevertheless 'actors' in the sense that they 'react' to the photo-

Girl Wearing a Flower in Her Hair. A photograph by Farsari, which he prominently displayed in one of his advertisements; it is frequently encountered in tourist albums. The flower is painted, and varies with each depiction, indicating perhaps that the painters had some freedom of design.

grapher. On the one hand this imbues the photograph with an unnatural feeling, but on the other it provides us with a sincere response of the Japanese of this period, who still considered photography a strange and wonderful medium. It is here that *shashin*, the 'reproduction of reality', entirely lives up to its name.

The colouring of photographs

A noteworthy feature of these tourist photographs is that they are hand-coloured. This technique, which was apparently introduced by Wirgman and Beato, became common in Japan from the 1880s onward. Although this practice occurred in the West as well it never reached the degree of sophistication it attained in Japan. Photographers in Japan were at a great advantage compared to their counterparts in the West. At their disposal were a pool of well-trained artisans, men who worked in the print shops producing woodblock prints. When lack of work in this field caused them to lose their jobs, the blooming photographic industry presented a new employment opportunity. Another reason for the success of Japanese photo-tinting is that, instead of the more opaque oil-based paints popular in the West, they used transparent, water-soluble pigments.

It is clear from Tamamura's advertising text above that it was not only photographers who could earn a reputation; artists could rise to fame as well. A well documented photo of 1867-68 of Felice Beato depicts a man, holding a palette and brush; it is entitled *My Artist*. Hand-colouring of photographs, when accurately done, is very labour-intensive. But Worswick's assertion that a skilled artisan could finish three at most in a twelve-hour workday,[58] seems improbable in view of the enormous output. The colour was very precisely added, generally in soft tones, although a harsh analine red characteristic of later Japanese woodblock prints also appears on later photos. Sometimes the artist added a little more than only colour, such as flowers in a girl's hair, or a cloud encircling Mount Fuji (no. 143)

The value of tourist photographs lies not only in the information they contain about Japan, but also in the artistic acumen they convey. They demonstrate the mastery of the photographer in composing the photograph and the virtuosity of the colouring artisans who, after all, were the same people who produced the woodblock prints whose technical perfection was so greatly admired in the West.

Albums

Photographs were collected in albums in much the same way that postcards were later. The album covers varied from simple cloth to silk brocade-lined covers or beautifully designed lacquer. Those with lacquer covers, the most expensive and the most desirable type of album, were especially produced by the traditional lacquer workshops. In order to protect the vulnerable lacquer surface these albums were often sold with Japanese-style cloth-covered boxes in which they could be stored. The size of photographs and albums varied: small albums contained photos from approximately 8.5 x 13.5 cms., larger photos were about 19 x 25 cms. The latter type was the most common and contained either 24 or 48 photos.

Albums were probably compiled both from photographs from one studio only, and from a selection from the different photo-shops. Some of the foreign residents in Japan, like Schilling, built up large collections comprising hundreds of these photographs. It was typical of the last decade of the nineteenth century that number and captions were added to the glass negative and printed together with the image. Customers would either look through sample books, ordering by number, or when visiting the studio chose the ones they fancied and had them put together in an album. Kimbei is known to have had an order-list of over 1,000 items, and at one point probably owned about 2,000 negatives.[59]

The various types of albums can be studied from price lists. For example, in 1892 Kimbei sold a dozen 8 x 10 inch coloured

Schilling used differend types of albums, nine of which are covered with a simple loosely woven, off-white fabric, on which the two characters for shashin *('photograph') are written.*
He kept his personal snapshots in a lacquer album.

photographs for $2 per dozen. The same size, but uncoloured, cost $1.50. The price of a lacquer covered album containing fifty of these photos was between $15 and $20, depending on the size of the cover. Photographs sold individually, the 8 x 10 inch coloured version sold at 20 cents each. Prints about twice this size (17 x 22 in.) were also available, at $2 each for the coloured version. The most expensive were the glass slides for the Magic Lantern; they costed $6 a piece. Uncoloured slides were half the price of the painted ones.[60]

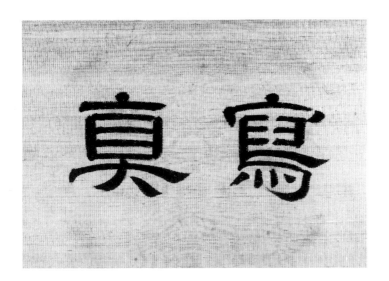

The problems of attribution

Regarding these tourist photographs, Handy justly states: 'Without firm attributions, one cannot offer complete art-historical interpretations of isolated images, whose meaning would be profoundly extended by the knowledge of the identity of the artist, his history and practice'.[61] However, at the same time, she and others also acknowledge the difficulty in determining authorship since many photographers did not leave a clear signature on their products. Photographers, unfortunately, were indifferent to whether a work was signed or not; to them photographs were mere commodities, 'a documentary image to be used for commercial purposes'.[62] And as with other merchandise, a photographer who bought negatives or stock from a colleague subsequently indicated these as his own. Nevertheless, clues to authorship can be found at different stages of the production process. First is the actual composition: the use and placement of props and the types of subjects can point to an individual photographer, as seen in Beato's distinctive use of a cameo to frame his subjects (page 23). Secondly, the negative, to which numbers and/or captions were frequently added, is important evidence for attribution. Thirdly, are the prints, the back of which sometimes contains valuable information. Finally, albums or books produced by photographic studios can provide another lead.

Although photographers differ in style, it is hazardous to rely exclusively on stylistic grounds in deciding authorship. This is especially so since with commercialization, popular 'designs' could be reproduced in very similar set-ups by several photographers. For example, *Bathing* (no. 11), is usually centred around one bath-tub, with five semi-nude women always engaged in similar activities, one in the bath, one taking care of the fire, etc. Nevertheless, clear differences can, with caution, be used in identification, as they have been in the case of Beato and von Stillfried. Beato is known for his unpolished, direct approach. He fancied natural scenes, travelled widely, and by means of photographs he recorded alluring as well as abhorrent aspects of this new and puzzling society. Von Stillfried preferred the controlled studio environment, and often made use of actors. His photographs were elegant artistic studies and his 'polished style is particularly unlike that of Beato, whose casual and animated figures are illustrative of social types more than they are portraits focusing on the inherent qualities of an individual'.[63] Rosin, besides noting divergences in style, also points to typical background attributes used by each and differences in the execution of their prints. For example, Beato often used a bamboo mat with typical zig-zag cord binding, while von Stillfried liked to have small stones or straw scattered on the ground and frequently seemed to have used some sort of backdrop (no. 49).[64] The background items are an aspect that deserves more careful attention. The same objects—certain paintings, folding screens and hanging scrolls—appear in a number of photographs. Probably photographs with the same background items were been made in one studio, if not by the same photographer. It is also worth considering the use of the same model for different photographs.

Of the criteria used in deciding the artist, negatives are the most helpful, by virtue of the numbers or captions attached to them. Unfortunately, even numbers or captions do not always indicate origin. Even if a certain system of numbering or titling can be associated with an individual photographer or studio, it is still not a totally reliable method of identification. Some photographers obtained negatives from others, as when Beato sold out to von Stillfried, whose business was later acquired by Farsari. Von Stillfried, for example, added small hand-written numbers to his photographs in order to identify them. But he added these to the negatives he bought from Beato as well.[65] Negatives were probably also exchanged or given away. The networks between photographers were intricate; many worked closely together with colleagues, either as teacher and pupil, or as partners. It is not difficult to find the same portrait with different captions. Sometimes buyers did not even bother to hide a former caption and added another one beside it, sometimes blackening the original inscription (no. 11). Another curiosity is found in sets of photographs apparently made one after another, but with dissimilar captions, as the Arashiyama photographs shown here. What happened in this case? Did two photographers go out to Arashiyama together, taking pictures of an almost identical scene? Or did one photographer shoot successive photographs, develop the negatives, keep one himself and transfer the other? These questions remain unanswered.

According to Robinson, photographers probably made copies of their own prints if the negative was damaged. And he mentions another practice: that of making a copy negative of a colleague's photograph, and adding their own name to it. For example, the famous photographs of the Meiji imperial couple, which are known to have been made by Uchida Kuichi, also exist mounted on von Stillfried's embossed matts.[66] The back of a print, or the matts on which they are mounted, can provide clues. For example, a substantial number of photographs in this book have four numbers, in Japanese, written in pencil on the reverse. These may correspond to an order list or catalogue and it is probably safe to assume that they derive from a single photographer, or at least were sold by one.

When no information has been added to the prints themselves but the photographs are part of an album, a rubber stamp or a label in that album can provide a clue. Nevertheless, there are pitfalls. Farsari's photo-albums contain prints not only from Beato or von Stillfried, but also from Kimbei and Ogawa Isshin.[67] A source that at first sight seems more reliable than albums randomly filled with prints, are the books published by the photographers. Beato's Views of Japan and Native Types can be relied on as reference material. But von Stillfried and Andersen published an album entitled Views and Costumes of Japan, in which of the 'types' reproduced many are Beato originals.[68] Japanese photographers have also issued their own collections of photographs, less well-known in the West, and individual photographs do turn up in tourist albums. For example, at least one of the earthquake photographs in this book (no. 165) was included in an album published in 1891, called Aiki shinsai shashin ('Photographs of the Aiki earthquake'), by Miyashita Kin.[69]

According to Handy, not being able to identify the artist would hamper the analysis of 'the precise extent of the compromises and conflicts between Western and Eastern pictorial traditions'.[70] Although the question of attribution is no doubt essential art historically, a strict division between artistic traditions of East and West is difficult to maintain since 'Meiji' was characterized by a moulding of Western traits to Japanese aesthetics. Her own article illustrates this issue. Handy describes a photograph, a Stillfried and Andersen studio imprint, as Two Young Women in a Conventional Western Pose, asserting that the sentimentality it exudes is derived from Western social and artistic conceptions, and that the photographer imposed Western ideas and poses on the two Japanese girls.[71] However, the same photograph can be found in Ozawa's Nihon no shashinshi, simply entitled Josei ('Women') and it is attributed to Ueno Hikoma. Ozawa says that, although Western pictorial traditions may have influenced Ueno's style, his portraits are nonetheless fine examples of Meiji photography.[72]

Road-side teahouses. *These photographs of Arashiyama, a popular resort for Kyoto residents, were apparently taken by the same photographer, a few seconds apart. However the different captions indicate that they were sold by different photo-shops.*

77 TEA HOUSE OF ARASHIYAMA

173 Arashiyama, Saikio

Photography and Japanese woodblock print tradition

Even before the introduction of photography, Japan already had a pictorial tradition of portraying aspects of daily life, as seen in the prints of the *ukiyo-e*. In spite of its foreign orientation, tourist photography possessed certain characteristics that are traceable to native art traditions, while at the same time exercising a strong influence on traditional Japanese art forms.

Photographs showing Japanese customs were intended for foreigners, but, the Japanese themselves also had earlier shown an interest in the seemingly strange customs of foreigners in the anonymous woodblock prints known as *Nagasaki miyage* ('Nagasaki souvenirs'). Before the opening of the country in the mid-nineteenth century, Japanese visiting Nagasaki could buy these prints as souvenirs, which depicted the domestic habits and appearances of the Chinese and Dutch. In some cases Western subjects, such as foreign women about which the Nagasaki Japanese had no direct knowledge, were also illustrated. These images were probably borrowed from Dutch engravings. From 1860 woodblock prints featuring foreigners in Yokohama *(Yokohama-e)* were produced in great numbers. The inexpensive medium of the woodblock print had long been a suitable means of recording documentary and topical subjects. With the *Yokohama-e,* 'now foreigners were news and the Japanese eagerly bought their pictures; some 800 separate designs of newcomers and their ways—fully eighty per cent of all Yokohama scenes - were issued during 1860 and 1861, despite the fact that there were only thirty-four Western merchants living in Yokohama in 1860 and no more than 100 to 200 by 1862'.[73]

Bijin ('beautiful women'), who were often well-known courtesans, were an important subject of *ukiyo-e.* In photography, too, portraits of famous geisha were popular, among Japanese as well as among foreigners. However, while foreigners apparently wanted images of anonymous 'Japanese women' as idealized in Western imagination, Japanese seem to have been interested in the portrayals of specific women they admired, and in this respect *bijin* photos were entirely in line with the woodblock print tradition. The trend in photography of depicting *bijin* is linked to the revival of the genre in woodblock prints by such artists as Toyohara Chikanobu, Ogata Gekkō (1859-1920) and Kobayashi Kiyochika (1847-1915) in the late nineteenth century. The style of portraiture is virtually identical in composition and atmosphere.

The 'famous views and places' genre, although popular with tourists, was not only intended to appeal to a foreign clientele. It is a continuation of the landscape theme popularized in woodblock prints. The approach to the subject in woodblock prints and photography did not differ greatly: whether the Japanese of the Edo period or the foreigners of the Meiji, the spots considered famous were largely the same. There was similarity in composition, too. For example, an element in close-up was placed against a distant scenic background. Iwasaki finds these similarities not surprising since some of the Japanese photographers, like Shimooka Renjō, were initially trained as painters, and Western photographers were frequently exposed to Japanese prints.[74]

There are still closer connections between photography and

woodblock prints. Kunisada IV designed two prints after the portraits of the Meiji empress and emperor made by Uchida Kuichi.[75] Although the faithful reproduction of composition and details in these prints clearly reveals their source, there was no intention to make them look like a photograph. In contrast, another woodblock print practice emerged in the Meiji period, which should be considered in the context of an important Meiji art tradition: that is the imitation of one art-form or technique in another. For example, special techniques were employed to make lacquer objects resemble stone, metal-work or paintings; and metal objects were given the appearance of lacquer. Thus woodblock prints were made to look like photographs, the foremost representative of this genre being Kobayashi Kiyochika. Throughout his artistic career, Kiyochika intermingled aspects of Western and Japanese traditions, a practice so characteristic of this period, and this is also evinced in his artistic training. Charles Wirgman introduced him to Western-style painting; Kawanabe Kyōsai (1831-1889) taught him traditional painting techniques; and Shimooka Renjō trained him in photography.[76]

The interaction of photography and woodblock prints is perhaps best represented by the printmaker Utagawa Yoshiiku (1833-1904). From 1870, as an increasing number of photographers established themselves in Tokyo, actor *buromaido* ('bromide') photographs depicting famous actors became very popular. Portrayals of famous actors had been perhaps most characteristic subject of the woodblock print, yet, Yoshiiku reacted to the photographic take-over by producing *ukiyo-e* that closely resembled the actor *buromaidos.* In doing so he set himself the difficult task of reproducing, by means of woodblocks, perspective, and the subtle shadows to be seen in photographs.

It is without doubt that the pictorial traditions of Japan were transformed by the introduction of photography. But it is also clear that Japanese pictorial traditions influenced the style and nature of photography. Nowhere else did the hand-colouring

The actor Ichikawa Sadanji I in a Shibaraku ('Wait a Moment') role; *from the series* Photographic Mirrors of Actors, (Haiyū shashin kagami), *1870, by Utagawa Yoshiiku. This print is a clear example of the imitation of photography by woodblock print artists in the latter nineteenth century.*

of photographs catch on as in Japan and this is clearly due to the existence of colour woodblock printing. The practice of producing images in quantity to sell to a wide public as memorabilia had been entrenched in Japanese culture for at least two centuries before the advent of photography.

Following the opening of Japan, the technology and culture of the West, which hitherto had been entering the country, albeit slowly, was introduced at a great pace. Photography arrived in Japan before the great wave of Westernization that marked the Meiji. After an initial period of hesitation, the Japanese eagerly adopted the photographic process and in the course of assimilation, they moulded the aesthetics of photography to their own pictorial traditions. Yet, in the initial stages of Japanese photography, Westerners played a crucial role as photographers and as customers. During this period, Westerners were curious to know more about exotic cultures and many set out to discover the unknown regions of the world. They either did so through actual expeditions or vicariously, through novels, plays, and the collecting of decorative objects which assisted their recreation of the exotic. The boom in Japanese tourist photography, therefore, should be seen against this setting of mutual curiosity, awe, and subsequent adaption. At the time of their production in the nineteenth century, these photographs were viewed only as souvenirs of a voyage or as a means to lose oneself in exotic fantasies. In this sense, the function of the photography was very similar to the medium of woodblock printing, from which photography derived so much in terms of subject matter and design. Naturally, of course, the fact that these photographs were geared towards foreigners—who had very specific expectations—dictated the fashion in which Japan was represented. Still, to dismiss these photographs as mere kitsch, does not do them justice and in the last decade Japanese scholars have begun to investigate their importance. Woodblock prints at the time of their production were seen simply as souvenirs and were little appreciated, yet today are highly valued throughout the world for their artistic achievement and historical significance. Simi-

larly, these photographs should also be seen, not only in terms of their technical accomplishment, but more importantly as documents of a period in Japanese history, when the country was undergoing tremendous social, cultural and political change. In this light, the Schilling collection is a poignant, romantic souvenir of a foregone age.

Notes

1. Ozawa, 1981, pp. 287, 296.

2. Seidensticker, 1985, p. 91.

3. For descriptions of the Rokumeikan and the Rokumeikan era, see Barr, 1968, pp. 12-3; Meech-Pekarik, 1986, p. 145ff; Seidensticker, 1985, pp. 97-100; Waley, 1984, pp. 31-2.

4. Matsumoto, 1985, p. 161-162; Meech-Pekarik, 1986, p. 100.

5. For changes in the outlook of the country and in personal attire, see Matsumoto, 1985; Meech-Pekarik, 1986, pp. 71-4, 98-9, 128-32.

6. Meech-Pekarik, 1986, p. 102.

7. Ozawa, 1986, p. 80.

8. Ives, 1974, pp. 20-21.

9. Quoted in Miner, 1958, p. 69.

10. Miner, 1958, p. 66.

11. Barr, 1968, p. 192.

12. Miner, 1958, pp. 47-9.

13. Loti, 1985, pp. 182-1823.

14. Miner, 1958, p. 47.

15. Hearn, 1984, pp. 161-163.

16. Meech-Pekarik, 1986, pp. 134-5.

17. Loti, 1985, p. 184.

18. Hearn, 1984, pp. 14-5.

19. Barr, 1968, p. 236

20. Adapted from Barr, 1968, illustrations.

21. Loti, 1985, p. 242.

22. Barr, 1968, p. 161.

23. Quoted in Meech-Pekarik, 1986, p. 132.

24. Actually, the first daguerreotype camera arrived in Japan in 1843. However, due to an oversight (Ozawa, 1981, p. 285), or because it was only sent to Ueno on approval (Moeshart, 1987a, p. 17), the camera was shipped back to Holland. Ueno had to wait until 1848 to really obtain his daguerreotype camera. There appears to have been some confusion as to the exact date of introduction of photography, for a treatment of this matter see Ozawa, 1981, pp. 285-6.

25. Moeshart, 1987a.

26. Ozawa, 1981, pp. 288, 291; Yokota, 1989, p. 188.

27. A solution of guncotton (nitrocellulose) in ether and alcohol. A solution of silver iodide and iron iodide was added to this collodion solution and the glass-plates were covered with a thin film of this mixture.

28. Moeshart, 1987a, pp. 22-3; Ozawa, 1981, pp. 293-4.

29. Dower, 1980, p. 9; Ozawa, 1981, p. 303.

30. Moeshart, 1987a, p. 23; Ozawa, 1981, p. 295.

31. Matsumoto, 1985, p. 159; Dower, 1980, p. 7.

32. Quoted in Edel, 1986, p. 16.

33. Loti, 1985, p. 17.

34. Loti, 1985, p. 151.

35. Loti, 1985, pp. 249-50. Reproductions of the photograph taken on that occasion in Edel, 1986, p. 31 and Ozawa, 1986, p. 90.

36. Ozawa, 1986, p. 94.

37. Dower, 1980, p. 7.

38. Ozawa, 1981, p. 300.

39. Kimura, 1985, p. 163; Ozawa, 1986, p. 94.

40. Quoted in Edel, 1986, p. 14.

41. Edel, 1986, p. 19.

42. Edel, 1986, pp. 12-20; Worswick, 1979, pp. 132-3; Saitō, 1987, pp. 175-84.

43. According to Edel, 1986, p. 23, Stillfried remained in Japan until 1883, when he sold out to Kimbei. Yokota (1989, shōjiten, p. 9) and Kimura (1985, p. 165) say that in 1885 he sold everything to Farsari, and that he left 'about the same time as Beato' (Kimura op. cit.).

44. Edel, 1986, p. 23; Worswick, 1979, p. 135; Banta, 1988, p. 12.

45. Robinson, 1988, p. 41.

46. Handy, 1988, p. 57.

47. Worswick, 1979, p. 144.

48. Kimura, 1985, p. 166; Yokota, 1989, shōjiten, p. 13; Saitō, 1990, pp. 227 and 230. Farsari's label is illustrated in Kimura, 1985, p. 166, and in Saitō, 1987, p. 186.

49. Kimura, 1985, p. 166; Saitō, 1987, p. 231; Yokota, 1989, shōjiten, p. 5.

50. Saitō, 1990, p. 231 and Yokota, 1989, p.

171. Could the ordering U.S. firm have been the Boston publishing firm Millet's who a year later published *Brinkley's Japan* which contained many original hand coloured photographs?

51. Adopted from Bennett, *Old Japan Catalogue.*

52. Saitō, 1990, pp. 228-30.

53. Robinson, 1988, p. 45.

54. Dower, 1980, p. 5.

55. Iwasaki, 1988, p. 32.

56. Daiichi Art Centre, 1985, p. 115. Loti's remark on photographs stuck on visiting cards, mentioned earlier, refers to this popular usage.

57. Dower, 1980, pp. 6-7.

58. Worswick, 1979, p. 143.

59. Saitō, 1990, p. 231; Yokota, 1989, pp. 171-2.

60. Saitō, 1990, p. 228.

61. Handy, 1988, pp. 55, 57.

62. Robinson, 1988, p. 41.

63. Handy, 1988, p. 57.

64. Rosin, 1987, pp. 34ff.

65. Rosin, 1987, p. 39.

66. Robinson, 1988, p. 41.

67. Kimura, 1985, p. 166; Robinson, 1988, p. 41. We came across a Farsari album which contained photographs of Kimbei (depicted in Worswick, 1979, p. 22) and of Ozawa Isshin (depicted in Daiichi Art Centre, 1985, p. 108).

68. Robinson, 1988, p. 41; Rosin, 1987 pp. 35-7.

69. Daiichi Art Centre, 1985, pp. 128-9.

70. Handy, 1988, p. 55.

71. Handy, 1988, p. 62.

72. Ozawa, 1986, p. 91.

73. Meech-Pekarik, 1986, p. 14.

74. Iwasaki, 1988, p. 29.

75. Depicted in Yokota, 1989, p. 192.

76. Jirka-Schmitz, 1990; Schaap, 1987, p. 132.

1646. Farmers carrying grass baskets

2. Carrying Woven Baskets, c. 1880. The baskets of these villagers are filled with mulberry leaves which are fed to silkworms. *Reference:* Illustrated in Ohara (1983), p. 81; no caption appears.

1584. Carrying children

R 6 Picking shell at Negishi, Yokohama.

8. Doctor. In this studio set-up, a *kanpōshi*, a doctor of the Chinese-style medicine, is taking the pulse of a patient. To his right are his medicine box wrapped in a decorative cloth *(furoshiki)* and his sword.

9. Carpenters. Workers using one-man saws are splitting timbers. Scenes of carpenters working were made famous by the woodblock print designer Hokusai in his view of carpenters in the *Thirty-six Views of Mount Fuji* (*Fūgaku sanjū rokkei,* c. 1830).

U 40. WAXING THE TREE.

10. Geisha Playing Games. Against a background of blooming wisteria these geisha are depicted playing a hide-and-seek game. This is a typical tourist photograph scene.

11. Bathing. Women portrayed in such scenes were a popular subject for studio photographers. The repetition of the title may point to a transfer of the negative from one studio to another.
Reference: For similar compositions, see Yokohama kaikō shiryōkan (1987), p. 207; Nihon sashinka kyōkai (1971), p. 66; and Daiichi Art Centre (1985), p. 93.

1547 Smoking tobacco

12. Women Around a Smoking Box. Tobacco was introduced to Japan by the Portuguese at the end of the sixteenth century and the custom became widespread, among men and women alike. The Japanese word, *tabako,* was adapted from the Portuguese *tabaco.* The tobacco pipe had a small bowl, permitting only one draw at a time.

13. Tattooed Man Pouring a Cup of Sake. *Irezumi* ('tattooing') has had a long history in Japan; the mention of tattooing first appears in the eighth century. During the course of its history, tattooing was used as a mark of punishment and in the Edo period it also became an exceedingly popular form of body decoration. Despite the sumptuary laws which sought to curb the practice, tattooing was still widespread when Japan opened its doors in the mid-nineteenth century. It was common among the lower ranks of society, particularly with professions like firemen, postmen, palanquin bearers and rickshaw drivers.

14. Samurai in Full Armour. The dramatic costumes of the samurai were, not surprisingly, a very successful subject for the tourist photographer.
Reference: in Iwasaki Yoshirō ikueikai (1989), pp. 138 & 166; the same group is illustrated in a slightly different pose. According to this source these photographs were also meant to serve as historical documents. They are attributed to the photographer Kitaniwa.

15. Curio Shop, c. 1880. Curio shops like this contained a wide selection of objects, ranging from dolls to furniture, and were a great attraction for foreigners.
Reference: Illustrated in Ohara (1983), p. 118.

16. Sumo. The origins of Sumo wrestling date to early in Japan's history, when its practice was imbued with religious symbolism. By the Edo period, however, Sumo was adapted as a popular form of entertainment and many images of Sumo tournaments and personalities have been perserved in *ukiyo-e* prints. Although at this time Sumo lost much of its religious significance, it, nonetheless, retained a number of ritualistic elements, such as the stamping of the players' feet and the throwing of salt. Before the tournament the participants appear in their expensive brocade *keshomawari*; in this photograph the name of one of the stables is printed in Roman script.

617. Festival Car at Kioto

17. Gion Festival, Kyoto. The Gion festival, still celebrated every July, is unique to Kyoto. It is an elaborate procession which trails through the city streets and is known for its colourful floats and ox-drawn carts. The cacophony of the celebration and music were meant to entertain and appease the *kami* ('diety'). In this photograph, the spectators are clad in both traditional and Western-style dress.

18. Courtesans and Attendants. This photograph portrays a group of prostitutes of the highest class *(tayū)* and their young attendants *(kamuro)* clad in resplendent kimono. The *kamuro* wear banners on their shoulders identifying them with their *tayū*. Unlike the lower-ranking prostitutes, *tayū* (later known as *oiran*) received extensive training in the various arts of entertainment — music and dance—and they were also much admired for their beauty. Due to their status, *tayū* were freer than other women in the pleasure quarters to reject potential clients. During assignations they were accompanied by their young attendants. The principal task of the *tayū* was to entertain and not necessarily to provide sexual services.

19. A Procession of *Tayū*. A view of the Shimabara pleasure
quarter of Kyoto at the time of the *hanakago* ('flower basket')
festival, which is held in spring.
Reference: Illustrated in Ohara (1983), p. 172.

20. Local Festival at a Shinto Shrine. The *mikoshi* ('portable Shinto shrine') carried in front of the building, the priests' robes, and the high poles with branches of the sacred *sakaki* tree, indicate that this is a Shinto ceremony. The traditional thatched shrine building provides an interesting contrast to the electric wires to the left and the brick building barely discernible to the right.

21. Palanquin. While the rickshaw gained popularity in the urban areas, the use of the palanquin held sway longer in rural terrain where rickshaw travel was unsuitable.

22. Urban Waterway. Before the Meiji period, the most important means of carrying goods of any size in Edo was via its waterways. Yet, as the historian Edward Seidensticker states, with the Meiji period that 'the city acquired wheels' and by 1926 most of the city's goods were transported overland.

24. Teahouse and Garden, Hikone, Shiga Prefecture. Hikone is located in the vicinity of Lake Biwa and the highway, Tokaido, and this view depicts a modest pavilion surrounded by a pond garden. Teahouses assumed a variety of forms, ranging from the architecture of the tearoom for the *chanoyu* ('tea ceremony') to more refined public pavilions as illustrated here. Gardens are an important element in the design of teahouses. The environment is greatly enhanced by the garden setting, as in this view. Other types of teahouses include simple wayside inns as well as those in the pleasure quarters which served as locations for assignations.

N 81 TEA-HOUSE GARDEN AT HIKONE.

26. Roadside Teahouse. A couple is busy preparing *kushi dango* ('rice-flour dumplings') which are placed on bamboo sticks and grilled on a wire rack. The woman seems to adhere to an older custom—shaved eyebrows and blackened teeth—that connotes conjugal status.

27. Man on Treadmill, c. 1890s. A farmer peddles a treadmill which is employed to flood the adjacent field before the transplantation of young rice plants.
Reference: Illustrated in mirror image, Ohara (1983), p. 88.

28. Pack-horse Chargers, c. 1880. In rural areas, the transportation of goods was left to semi-specialists called 'pack-horse chargers' *(dachin mochi).*
Reference: Illustrated in Ohara (1983), p. 82; no caption appears.

669 Köriyama Village near Nara.

29. Koriyama Village near Nara. A view of wet-field farming.

30. Children. Babies were normally carried in slings slung across the back.

31. Harvesting Bamboo Shoots. These highly prized delicacies are collected in mid-April.

1647 Making straw mats.

32. Weaving Tatami Mats. Two men are pictured weaving a tatami mat, which consists of a thick straw base and thin reed covering. It was and still is the principal type of floor covering.

34. Gathering Tea Leaves at Uji, Yamashiro. Tea from the Uji district in Yamashiro (now part of Kyoto prefecture) is particularly well-known.

1586 Spinning cotton.

33. Spinning Cotton. An elderly couple at work; the woman is handling a small hand-spinner.

35. Cormorant Fishing on the River, Nagaragawa, Gifu. Using trained cormorants to catch fish is not as efficient as line or net fishing, but is certainly more spectacular. The bird is held on a rein and collared; the thin collar prevents the cormorant from swallowing any fish. The event is still a popular tourist attraction and here a pleasure boat is pictured in the background.

36. Fishermen with their Cormorants, Tamagawa, Hachiōji.

37. Line Fishing in the Tamagawa.

38. Japanese Fishermen, c. 1890. This type of Japanese boat was used for fishing in calmer waters like bays and the Inland Sea.
Reference: Illustrated in Ohara (1983), p. 112; the caption reads 'Five-oar fishing boat on the Inland Sea' and the following note states that manning a boat with five oars was rare.

39. Gathering Shellfish. At low tide shellfish could be gathered from the seashore and it was an additional source of income for the fishermen and their families. Gathering was primarily done by women.

40. Lower-ranking Prostitutes, Yoshiwara. Many prostitutes came from very poor families who would sell their children to brothels, often to pay off debts.

41. Carpenters Preparing House Beams. Carpenters are busy plying their trade; noteworthy is the man in the foreground who is using a *sumitsubo* ('ink pot') to mark dimensions.
Reference: Illustrated in Ohara (1983) p. 133; the author suggests that the man with the top-knot to the left was probably added by the photographer to complete the composition.

1589 Carpenters.

42. Girl Playing a Shamisen. A set-up image in which a girl plays a *shamisen* (three stringed lute) with a plectrum.

43. Bathing. A bathing scene not made in the studio; the distortion of the child's face indicates the long exposure required for the photograph.

44. Cooking. The deliberate placement of the compositional elements and the positions of the subjects belies a studio set-up.

45. Craftsmen Eating Soba. Workmen are enjoying a meal of *soba*, (a type of buckwheat noodle) from stacked lacquered boxes. Photographs of such 'workmen meals' were common; yet, the addition of the caption 'Eating Macaroni' makes this image especially intriguing.

46. Komusō. Mendicant Zen priests *(komusō)* of the Fuku sect, customarily wore a hood made of sedge which concealed their faces. In the seventeenth century the sect was granted exclusive rights by the shogunal government to play the *sakuhachi* (bamboo flute). In 1871 the Meiji government abolished this law and *sakuhachi* playing became a secular entertainment.

47. Buddhist Priest. High ranking priests were permitted to use scarlet, purple and light green in their robes. A studio set-up, this image is also interesting with the portrayal of Mount Fuji on a painted backdrop.

48. Buddhist Priest with Young Apprentices.

49. Buddhist Pilgrims. Pilgrims travelled throughout Japan, visiting sacred places and offering prayers to travellers and residents. Photograph by von Stillfried.
Reference: Illustrated in Ozawa (1990), p. 225.

C 98. PILGRIMS.

50. Buddhist Pilgrims. These pilgrims carry *zushi* ('portable shrines'), which held images, as seen here, of the bodhisattva Jizō. Jizō, a popular saint, is the saviour of small children, the patron of travel as well as the protector of pregnant women.

51. Ainu Couple. The Ainu peoples inhabit the northernmost Japanese island, Hokkaido. Racially unrelated to the modern Japanese, they lived in virtual isolation until the nineteenth century. Their clothing is unique as is the practice by women of tattooing around their mouths.

52. Farmers Wearing Rain Coats. A *mino* (straw raincoat) and *kasa* (hat made of bamboo or sedge), was traditionally worn by farmers and street vendors as protection against inclement weather.

53. Basket and Broom Peddlers. Transient peddlers, who sold a variety of goods, from vegetables to flowers, noodles to books, were a common sight in Edo-period Japan.

54. Candy Vendor. A staged photograph of a vendor blowing various shapes out of *shinko*, a dough made from ground rice. *Reference:* A similar view is illustrated without the young boy, in Ohara (1983), p. 128.

55. Bamboo Vendor. Set against a painted backdrop of a rural village, a young women, in a rather stayed pose, points at the bamboo shoot offered to her by the vendor.

56. Insect Vendor. Set against a painted backdrop of a rural scene, the kiosk of an insect salesman is filled with delicately carved wooden cages for insects *(mushikago).* These cages housed insects such as cicadas, which were much admired for their melodious song.

57. Green Grocer. A realistic view of a *yaoya* ('vegetable shop') packed with a diversity of vegetables such as bamboo shoots, daikon and mushrooms.

58. Porcelain Shop. This type of shop was called a *setomonoya* ('shop of Seto objects'), named after the Seto area in Aichi prefecture, an important centre of ceramic production since the medieval period. *Setomono* became a generic appellation for ceramics.

59. Dry Goods Store. In this studio photograph, two women are purveying bolts of brightly coloured fabrics; the merchant to the right is using an abacus.

60. Furniture Dealer. View of a typical commercial street, lined with shops of various sorts; the shop of a furniture merchant in the foreground is filled to the brim with goods.

42. A DEALER IN FURNITURE.

61-63. Sumo. The match comprises four minutes of preliminary ritual (61) and is followed by a wrestling bout which lasts on average thirty seconds. The goal is to force the opponent out of the circle marked by straw bags, or to have him touch the floor of the *dohyō* ('ring') with any part of the body other than the feet. While winning techniques are varied, it is important to be able to have a good grip on the opponent's belt *(mawashi)*. During tournaments the *sagari,* an apron of strings made from twisted and starched silk strips, hangs from this belt (62). The *gyōji* ('referee') stands near the wrestlers, while the *shinpan* ('judge') sit next to the pillar of the *dohyō* (63).

62.

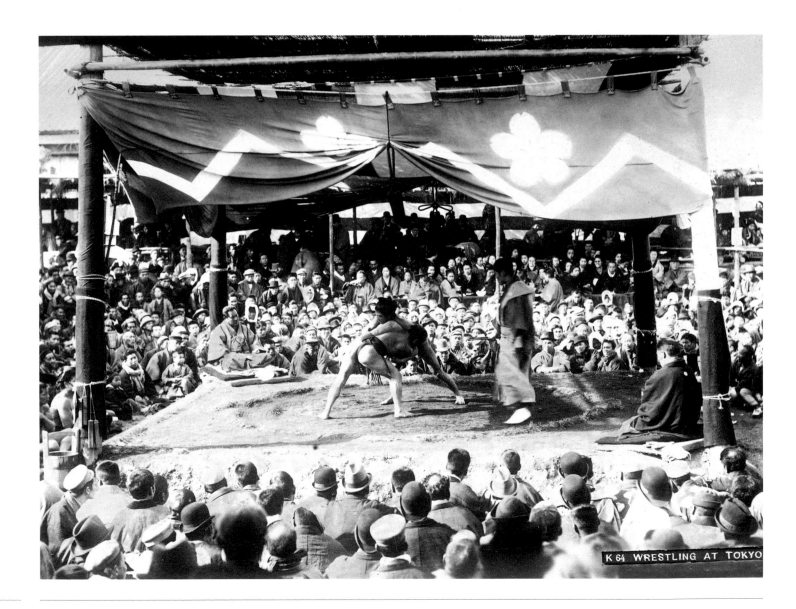

K 64 WRESTLING AT TOKYO

64. Mikoshi. *Mikoshi* are portable Shinto shrines which house the spirit of the diety. During Shinto festival processions, they are carried through the streets of the shrine community. This photograph illustrates a smaller *mikoshi* carried by children.

65. Shrine Visit. An *omiyamairi* ('shrine visit') is the first visit of a baby to its tutelary shrine and it generally occurs 3-4 weeks after birth. Relatives and friends present *inu hariko* ('papier-mâché dogs') to the child as a symbol of protection and good health.

66-68. Festival Procession. A group of samurai (66) wearing swords and kimono-clad young women (67) posing before what appears to be a local secular festival procession (68). Perhaps more intriguing than the groups which were the objects of these photographs is the garb of the spectators. The women are clad in kimonos, while the men have adopted Western-style dress in varying degrees. Western-style hats were worn with both Japanese and Western clothing, and their diversity is surprising. As is seen here, various fashions co-existed in both Western and Japanese clothing styles. To the left in (66) appears a representative example of the Meiji Japanese outfit: a Western hat, combined with kimono and *hakama* (a divided skirt) over which a *haori* (Japanese-style coat) is worn.

68. Festival Procession. It is interesting that a traditionally-clad man in the foreground carries a standard which is decorated with the crest of the Tokugawa family. Behind him, among the onlookers, is a uniformed man with a Western-style drum which is decorated with Meiji symbols: the *hinomaru,* a red circle representing the sun, which is set against a white background. The *hinomaru* became the official symbol for Japan's flag in 1870. The 'radiant sun', depicted to the right on the drum, came to denote the imperial household; it was an ingenious elaboration on the sun design, on the one hand, and the sixteen-petalled chrysanthemum crest, traditionally representing the imperial family, on the other.

69. Parade of Fire Brigades at New Year. Fires were a frequent occurrence in Japan and they were often devastating. In Edo, conflagration was so common that fires earned the sobriquet, *Edo no hana* ('Flowers of Edo'). During the New Year's celebrations, the members of the various brigades gathered together, bedecked in their groups' costumes, and performed stunts on high ladders for expectant viewers. A row of *matoi* ('firemen standards'), which represented—both carved and painted—crests of the individual groups is visible in the background. To the right is a *yagura* ('watchtower'). These towers could be up to 9 metres high and were permanently manned. When a fire was discovered, a huge drum was beaten; the rhythm would indicate the distance and location of the blaze.

70. Funeral Procession. A funeral in Japan is almost always a Buddhist ceremony.

71. Palanquin. The *kago* ('palanquin') was an important means of transport during the Edo period. The simplest type is seen here and consists of a bamboo seat suspended from a long pole hoisted on the shoulders of two men. The two carriers in this studio photo display the full designs of their *happi* coats.

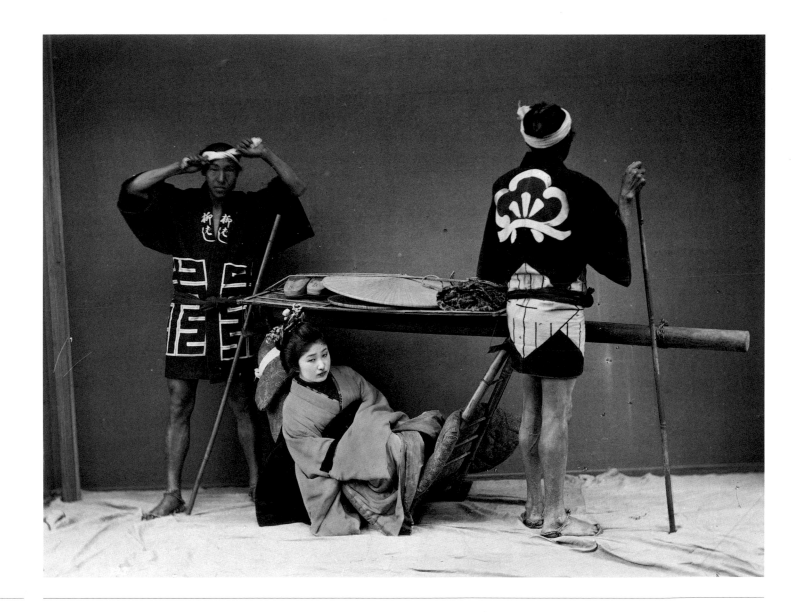

72. Rickshaw, Tokyo. A view of rickshaw on the grounds of the temple and Tokugawa tutelary Shinto shrine, Sannōji, in Akasaka, Tokyo, during the cherry blossom season. In the background, three uniformed officers are looking on with interest.

73-74. Views on the River, Sumidagawa. The Sumidagawa flows through eastern Tokyo and empties into Tokyo Bay. During the history of the city, first as Edo and later as Tokyo, the river was an necessary artery for the carriage of goods. However, it was additionally a popular route for pleasure boats which catered to geisha and their entourages as well as delivering passengers to the pleasure quarters of the Yoshiwara, located a short distance from the river's banks.

74. Pleasure Boats on the Sumidagawa river.

75. Rickshaw, Yokohama. The *jinrikisha* ('human powered vehicle') was invented in Japan around 1868. By the 1870s, their use was widespread, precipitating the disappearance of the palanquin and boat as a method of personal transport. The English term rickshaw is a corruption of the Japanese word.

76. Ox Carts. Prior to the introduction of trains, ox- and horse-carts were the major means of overland transportation.

77. Yakatabune, Kanazawa near Yokohama. House-shaped boats (*yakatabune*) were utilized for pleasure trips and the passengers could enjoy the view seated in a small cabin. It is said that the boatmen should maneuver the boat in such a manner so as to not spill the sake of his passengers.

78. Japanese Junk. The Yamato ('Japan') type of cargo vessel anchored in the Enoura inlet in Suruga Bay, Shizuoka prefecture. During Japan's long period of seclusion, it was strictly forbidden to leave the country and at this time all European-style ships and seaworthy Japanese vessels were destroyed. Only smaller ships such as this coastal junk remained.

Reference: Illustrated in Ohara (1983), p. 113.

1073 Enoura, Numadzu.

79. Roadside Teahouse at Nikko. Travel along routes between the major urban centres increased during the Edo period and many thoroughfares were dotted with roadside teahouses, where the travellers could enjoy a cup of tea and have a smoke before continuing on their journey. This picture illustrates several types of rural travellers like farmers and palanquin bearers.

61 Ogurayama, Nikkō.

80. Room at an Inn, Hakone. This photograph illustrates an interior with a number of elements characteristic of traditional Japanese domestic architecture such as the decorative alcove *(tokonoma)*, sliding wall-and-door panels *(fusuma)*, and the wooden post-and-beam construction. Only the addition of electric ceiling lamps hint at Western influence.

M 65. THE ROOM OF HOT-SPRING PLACE, HAKONE.

81. Room at a Teahouse, Yumoto. The *tokonoma* was reserved for the display of treasured objects such as *kakemono* ('hanging scroll'), an appropriate seasonal flower arrangement or a bonsai. The alcove of the papered lattice window to the right is also a vestige of an earlier domestic architectural tradition. Yumoto was a hot spring resort in the Hakone area.

82. Tokonoma. The eclectic display in this rather grand *tokonoma* is further accentuated by the knarled posts of the *tokobashira*, the supports flanking the alcove space. The most highly prized trees were generally reserved for the position of *tokobashira* and as seen here they are left unhewn in order to display the natural beauty of the wood.

83. Teahouse Room. The careful display of musical instruments in the foreground include a *koto* (13-stringed cyther), two *shamisen*, a *tsuzumi* (hand-drum) and a *shimedaiko* (tunable drum). The view into this unoccupied room, the deliberate arrangement of the instruments and the opened shoji, which offers a glimpse of the garden, create a feeling of calm and anticipation.

1020 Musical Instruments, Tea House Room.

P. 35 WHISPERING

87. Geisha. Catering to foreign taste various 'Japanese' items have been placed together in this photo. One girl holds a fan, another serves tea and a third is filling her pipe from a tobacco pouch.

Photographic portraits were very popular with the Japanese in the Meiji period; it was common to exchange them with friends as a keepsake. The images were also printed on a small scale (8.3 x 5.4 cm.) and used as calling cards. This type of photograph often portrayed geisha, who were idolized in much the same way as well-known actors, and whose portraits were also very much in demand.

93A

92-93. Portraits of two women. The settings combine elements associated with Japan such as the women's distinctive kimonos and hairdoes, or props like lanterns and chrysanthemums, with a sentimentality that must have appealed to Western sensibilities.

94. Back View of Two Women. This photograph may appear odd, however, it gives a clear view of the knot of the *obi* (the kimono sash) and the elaborate hair decorations.

95. Girls Reading a Book. A group of girls, surrounded by cherry blossoms, appear engrossed in reading a book. This is a typical souvenir photo scene, although the Western-style chair in the right corner seems out of place.

96-101. Portraits of Individual Women. Western aesthetics and the creative possibilities offered by photographic techniques clearly influenced the style of these photographs.

98.

99.

102-104. Laughing Geisha. Photographs such as these were quite exceptional in expression and they were probably attuned to the taste of Western visitors. They successfully capture the exuberance of the smiling young girl, a decided contrast to the usual female portraits which are more contemplative, serene and idealized. The jovial young girl of these photographs was apparently quite popular as she is encountered frequently in similar poses in tourist albums.

103.

105-110. Views of Mount Fuji. In the West, Mount Fuji is perhaps the sight most immediately associated with Japan. A semi-active composite volcano, it last erupted in 1707, and even Edo, situated some 100 kilometres to the southwest, was covered with ashes. Fuji has been the object of religious veneration from at least as early as the Heian period (794-1185), when pilgrims climbed the mountain as part of their religious praxis. By the Edo period, climbing Mount Fuji and other mountains like it, was practiced by the believers of the Shugendo sect and others. Mount Fuji was not only the centre of a religious cult, but was also the subject of many Japanese paintings and prints, the most famous being the print series *Thirty-six Views of Mount Fuji* by Hokusai. This photograph shows Mount Fuji from Enoshima, west of Kamakura.

106. Mount Fuji from Taganoura, Shizuoka prefecture.

605 HAKONE

112. View of the Nakamise dōri. The Nakamise dōri ('Street of Inside Shops') was so called because these shops stand within the precincts of a temple, the Asakusa Kannonji (or Sensōji) in Tokyo. The row of two-storied Western-style red-brick buildings was constructed in 1885. This particular view depicts a clocktower in the far left, which was constructed in 1892. Another tower, erected in the area in 1894, is not yet visible, indicating that this photograph may have been taken around 1893. Interesting in this image are the group of rickshaw in the foreground, serving as it were as the Meiji equivalent of the modern-day 'taxi-stand'.

Reference: **Illustrated in Yokohama kaikō shiryōkan (1990), p. 83.**

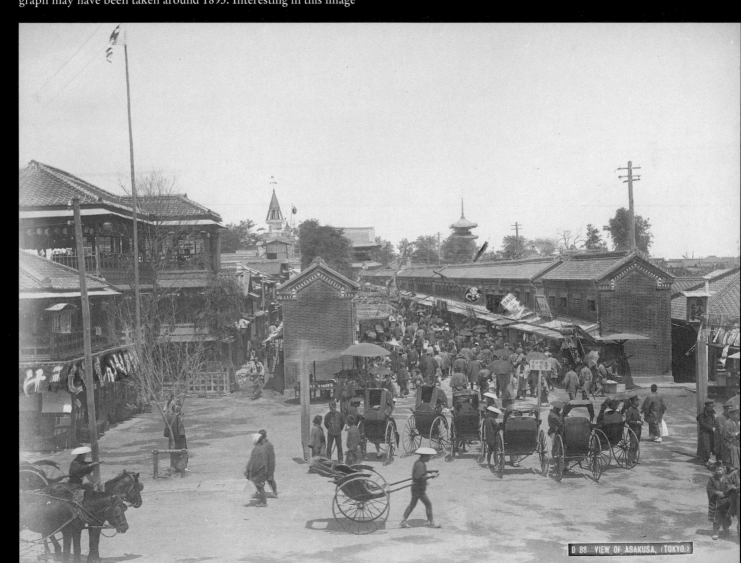

D 88 VIEW OF ASAKUSA, (TOKYO.)

X 73 THEATER STREET AT TOKYO

114. The 'Twelve Stories', Asakusa. Designed by the British engineer William K. Barton and completed in 1890, the 'Twelve Stories' was perhaps the most conspicious Western-style structure in Meiji Tokyo. It housed the first elevator in Japan—imported from the United States— and shops inside sold goods from all over the world. The building suffered structural damage in the 1894 earthquake, after which time it was reinforced with a steel frame; nevertheless, the upper four stories were destroyed by the Great Kanto Earthquake of 1923. Eventually the building was demolished.

115-116. Views of the Yoshiwara. The Yoshiwara was established in 1617 as a licensed quarter for the entertainment of the mercantile population. In 1657, the district was moved to the present-day Taito ward in Akasaka and renamed Shin Yoshiwara ('New Yoshiwara'). During the final century of the Edo period, Yoshiwara came to be the cultural centre of the Edo mercantile class. In 1900 a law was issued permitting the free movement of licensed prostitutes. As a result many courtesans established themselves in other parts of the city and Yoshiwara's prominence as the centre of entertainment and culture gradually declined. The Yoshiwara was formally disbanded in 1958, when prostitution was outlawed. These views date from the last decade of the nineteenth century, as witnessed by the appearance of electric lighting.

117-118. Views of Ginza. After the Great Fire of 1872, the then unsophisticated Ginza was completely rebuilt with Western-style two-storied red-brick buildings and thereafter epitomized the 'new' image of Tokyo. From 1882 to 1903, horse-drawn trolleys operated between Nihonbashi and Shimbashi; they were later replaced by electric trams. In the background of (117) stands the Hattori clocktower, which was built in 1894. No.118 shows another clocktower in the right foreground which was erected in 1876. The area is a maze of telegraph wires. (c. 1900)
Reference: (118) Illustrated in Ohara (1983), pp. 34-5.

118.

Iris garden at Horikiri Tokyo

1004 STREET OF YOKOHAMA.

725. View of Kobe.

124. View of Kobe. As a free port, Kobe was younger than the treaty port of Yokohama, and foreigners were a less common sight. In 1880, there were about two hundred and fifty Westerners resident in Kobe, while Yokohama at that time had about one thousand.

1065 NAGOYA TOWN

125. View of Nagoya. Located on the southern coast of Honshu, and between Kyoto and Tokyo, Nagoya was the seat of the Owari branch of the Tokugawa family. As a result, the city became an important cultural and commercial centre in the Edo period.

864 Kiyomidzu Temple, Kiōto.

on fire. It was rebuilt in 1955. Both the building and the garden are well-known for their beauty.

155 Maruyama Saikin

132. Nikko, Tochigi prefecture. The village of Nikko is possibly most famous for the Nikko Tōshōgū, the mausoleum of the first Tokugawa shogun, Ieyasu (1542-1616). A sacred bridge, the Shinkyo bashi, leading from the nearby village to the shrine grounds, spans the river, Daiyagawa, and it contrasts an adjacent wooden bridge (158). The print designer Kobayashi Kiyochika (1847-1915) illustrated a similar view in his series, *Views of Famous Sights of Japan* (*Nihon meisho zue*, 1897). The lacquered bridge, *mihashi*, was erected in the 1630s and was initially opened only to a select few and on designated festival days.

3 Sacred Bridge, Nikkō.

20 Karamon Iyeyasu Temple, Nikkō

20 Revolving Lantern, Nikkô.

73 Daiya river. Nikkō.

136. The islands of the Inland Sea. Situated between Honshu and Shizuoka prefecture, the Inland Sea was not only a significant transportation route, but also an area renowned for its beauty. It is said to contain nearly 300 islands of which the island of Awajishima is the largest and easternmost.

R 89 Awajishima (Inland sea)

137-138. Torii of the Utsukushima Shrine, Miyajima, Inland Sea. Miyajima ('Shrine Island'), situated south-west of Hiroshima, is famous for its shrines and its scenery. The *torii*, which marks the entrance to a shrine's sacred ground, is the largest such gate in Japan.

778 Portal Miyajima, Inland Sea

777 Kintai Bridge, Iwakuni.

139. The Bridge, Kintaikyō. The Kintaikyō ('Silver Brocade Sash Bridge') is unusual as it was built without using nails, a feature rarely found in Japanese architecture. Crossing the river, Nishikigawa, in Iwakuni, Suō province (present-day Yamaguchi prefecture), the original bridge was built in 1673. It was destroyed by a flood in 1950 and later reconstructed; even today it is still a popular tourist attraction.

140. Cherry Blossoms, Yoshir

Yoshino has historically been
noted for its cherry blossoms,
its legendary beauty has inspir
numerous poems:

'Flowering cherries,
Blossoming in the mountains
Of fair Yoshino....'
(*Shinsen haka,* 10th century)

932 CHERRY BLOSSMS YOSHINO

141. Mount Fuji from Kawaibashi, Gifu Prefecture.
Reference: See Ozawa(1990), p. 69; this version was taken by Farsari and depicts the same location except that a farmhouse appears on the right.

142. Mount Fuji from Omiya Village, Shizuoka Prefecture. Photograph by Kusakabe Kimbei.
Reference: Illustrated in Yokohama kaikō shiryōkan (1990), p. 109.

143. Mount Fuji from Iwabuchi, Shizuoka Prefecture. A cloud encircling the top of the mountain was added by the painter.

144. Ōjigoku, Hakone. A view of Ōjigoku ('Big Inferno') where steam is seen eminating from the geyser.

234-B OJIGOKU HAKONE

145. The Hotel Fujiya, Miyanoshita. The Fujiya was built in 1878 and was the first Western-style building to be erected in the Hakone district. Representative of the eclecticism of Meiji architecture, the majestic hotel combines a heavy-tiled Japanese roof with the open lattice-work of a Western-style wooden building. Miyanoshita was popular for its scenery, climate and hot-springs. This photograph is by Farsari.
Reference: Illustrated in Yokohama kaikō shiryōkan (1990), p. 61.

E 8. FUJIYA MIYANOSHITA.

146. Ochanomizu, Jimbōchō, Tokyo. View of a bridge over the river, Kandagawa, at Ochanomizu ('Tea Water'). The site was so named after the water from a spring here which was said to be used for the tea of the second Tokugawa shogun, Hidetada (1579-1632).

148. Imperial Palace Bridge, Tokyo. One of the bridges leading to the Imperial Palace which is situated on the grounds of the earlier Edo Castle.
Reference: Illustrated in Yokohama kaikō shiryōkan (1990), p. 69.

147. Museum at Kudanzaka, Tokyo. Located on the grounds of the Yasukuni shrine, this unusual, still extant, brick structure was designed by the Italian G.V. Cappelletti and built in 1882. It served as a military exhibition hall.

149. View of Ginza, Tokyo. Festive red and white decorations and stalls dot the street.

150. The Bridge, Shimbashi, Tokyo. The iron bridge illustrated here was constructed in 1899 to serve the increasingly heavy trolley traffic. It replaced an earlier wooden structure.

151. Akasaka Park in the Cherry Blossom Season. After the turn of the century, Akasaka rivalled Shimbashi as an important entertainment centre. Akasaka's teahouses were frequented by businessmen and politicians whose offices were located nearby.

152-153. The Ōgiya, Ōji. Founded in 1648, the Ōgiya was a well-known teahouse in Ōji, a northern suburb of Edo and located in the vicinity of the Sumidagawa. Known for its cherry blossoms and picturesque riverain setting, Ōji had been a popular locale for outings and picnics for the city's residents.
Reference: Photographs of this same teahouse and garden, in Edel (1986), p. 60-1; Hoerner (1985), p. 32; Ozawa (1990), p. 34; Yokohama kaikō shiryōkan (1990), pp. 94-5.

154-155. Mukōjima. The Mukōjima ('Island on the Other Side') was another area for pleasure excursions. With its many temples and teahouses, the island, which bordered the Sumidagawa, was especially popular among artists and writers in the nineteenth century. At the end of the century however, Meiji politicians and businessmen were also coming to the area, building luxurious villas and gardens.

156. Cherry blossoms at Koganei. This view depicts the upper banks of the river, Tamagawa, in southwest Tokyo, resplendent with blooming cherry trees. A noted site for excursions by Edo and later Tokyo commoners, a group of uniformed men pose here for the photographer.

157-159. Views of Yokohama. After its designation as a treaty port in 1859, the city of Yokohama became the most important of the free ports. It was also the centre of Meiji tourist photography. In the foreground of (157) is the native sector of the city, characterized by the wooden-framed Japanese-style architecture, while across the river to the right is the Western settlement. This section of Yokohama was constructed with Western-style stone and brick buildings. Japanese-style houses, bordering the sector, are seen in (158); one carries the sign in English reading 'Curio Store'. The main street of the city (159) was occupied by Western-style buildings such as the Post Office (right foreground) of 1889 and the Public Office for the inspection of silk threads (left foreground) which dates from 1896. A clocktower from 1874 is also visible.

160. Shijō dōri, Kyoto. The Shijō dōri is the main street of the Gion district. To the left is the characteristic watchtower and to the right a sign (reversed) reads *shashin* ('photograph'), no doubt indicating a photographer's studio.

161. The Bridge, Sanjō ōhashi, Crossing the River, Kamogawa, Kyoto. This bridge was reconstructed in 1881; however, the area under the bridge remained unchanged and continued to serve as a refuge for the outcastes class. Houses and *kura* ('storehouse') dot the background.

162. The Bridge, Shijō ōhashi, Kyoto. The bridge was rebuilt in 1874 using iron; the supporting pillars, nevertheless, attempt to recreate a wooden construction. In the background are typical examples of *machiya* ('town house').

163-165. Aiki Earthquake. Early in the morning of 28 August, 1891, a severe earthquake struck Central Japan in Aichi and Gifu prefectures. More than 7,000 persons were killed and 17,000 wounded. Over 140,000 buildings, both of traditional and Western style, were destroyed; the force of the quake is also apparent in the bent railroad ties and rails (165). Photographs may be attributable to Miyashita Kin.

Reference: (165) Illustrated in Daiichi Art Centre (1985), p. 129, and attributed to Miyashita Kin.

166. Ganman Road, Nikko. The environs of the Ganman'en (Ganman Pool), in the river Daiyagawa, was one of the famous views of Nikko. This view of the site includes a waterwheel and was probably taken by Farsari, c. 1880.
Reference: Illustrated in Ozawa (1990), p. 80.

167. Chūzenji Lake. The Nikko region also included a number of resort sites such as the Chūzenji lake, where Japanese and foreigners alike went to escape the sultry Tokyo summers.

168. Furōjima, Matsushima. Matsushima Bay, in Miyagi prefecture, is reputed to have 260 islands, many in unusual shapes and many covered with pine trees. Together with the Itsukushima Shrine in the Inland Sea and Amanohashidate in Kyoto prefecture, the region is traditionally counted as one of the three most beautiful spots in Japan.

169. Miyajima and The Utsukushima Shrine, Inland Sea. Originating in the sixth century, the shrine is positioned on the island shore and during high tide, the magnificient *torii* and main sanctuary are surrounded by water.

Bibliography

Andon, Bulletin of the Society for Japanese Arts and Crafts/1990
Special issue publishing the proceedings of a symposium on Meiji arts at the Leiden Museum of Ethnology, May 1987. Leiden: Society for Japanese Arts and Crafts.

Banta, Melissa /1988
"Life of a Photograph: Nineteenth-Century Photographs of Japan from the Peabody Museum and Wellesley College Museum", *A Timely Encounter,* etc. see Banta and Taylor, 1988, pp. 11-21.

Banta, Melissa and Susan Taylor (eds.) / 1988
A Timely Encounter. Nineteenth-Century Photographs of Japan. Cambridge, MA., Peabody Museum Press and Wellesley, MA., Wellesley College Museum.

Barr, Pat / 1968
The Deer Cry Pavilion. A Story of Westerners in Japan 1868-1905. New York: Harcourt, Brace & World Inc.

Colombo, Attilio and Isabella Doniselli / 1980
De Japanse fotografie van 1848 tot heden. Amsterdam: Contact.

Daiichi Art Centre (ed.) / 1985
Shashin no makuake [The Dawn of Photography], vol. 1 of *Nihon shashin zenshū* [The Complete Collection of Japanese Photography]. Tokyo: Shōgakukan.

Dower, John W. / 1980
"Ways of Seeing, Ways of Remembering. The Photography of Prewar Japan", *A Century of Japanese Photography.* Japan Photographers Association, ed. New York: Pantheon Books, pp.1-20.

Edel, Chantal / 1986
Once Upon a Time. New York: Friendly Press.

Galeries nationales du Grand Palais, Paris & Musée nationale d'art occidentale, Tokyo (eds) / 1988
Le Japonisme. Paris: Editions de la Réunion des musées nationaux.

Handy, Ellen / 1988
"Tradition, Novelty and Invention: Portrait and Landscape Photography in Japan, 1860-1880s", *A Timely Encounter,* etc. see Banta and Taylor, 1988, pp. 53-69.

Hearn, Lafcadio / 1984
Japan: An Attempt at Interpretation. Rutland, VT. and Tokyo: Charles E. Tuttle Co. (first edition published in New York in 1904).

Hibbett, Howard / 1975
The Floating World in Japanese Fiction. Rutland, VT. and Tokyo: Charles E. Tuttle Co.

Hoerner, Ludwig / 1985
Eine Fotoreise durch das Alte Japan. Dortmund: Harenberg.

Ives, Colta Feller / 1974
The Great Wave: The Influence of Japanese Woodcuts on French Prints. New York: The Metropolitan Museum of Art.

Iwasaki, Haruko / 1988
"Western Images, Japanese Identities: Cultural Dialogue between East and West in Yokohama Photography", *A Timely Encounter,* etc. see Banta and Taylor, 1988, pp. 23-37.

Iwasaki Yoshirō ikueikai [Scholarship Society of Iwasaki Yoshirō] (ed) / 1989
Shashinshū: Meiji no Yokohama-Tokyo: nokosarete ita garasu kanban kara [Photographic Collection: Meiji-period Yokohama and Tokyo from extant glass plates]. Yokohama: Kanazawa shinbunsha.

Jirka-Schmitz, Patrizia/1990
'Trompe-l'oeil, simulation and imitation in the decorative arts of the Meiji period', *Andon* etc. see Andon 1990, pp. 73-85.

Kimura, Yasuo / 1985
"Gaikokujin shashinka to Yokohama shashin" [Foreign Photographers and Yokohama Photography], *Shashin no makuake,* see Daiichi Art Centre, 1985, pp. 163-6.

Loti, Pierre / 1985
Japan: Madame Chrysanthemum. London: KPI Ltd (first French edition by Calmann-Levy, titled *Madame Chrysanthème,* published in Paris in 1887).

Matsumoto, Tokuhiko / 1985
"Bunmei kaika no naka no shashin" [Photography in the 'Civilization and Enlightenment' period], *Shashin no makuake,* see Daiichi Art Centre, 1985, pp. 159-162.

Meech-Pekarik, Julia / 1986
The World of the Meiji Print: Impressions of a New Civilization. New York and Tokyo: Weatherhill.

Miner, Earl / 1958
The Japanese Tradition in British and American Literature. Princeton: Princeton University Press.

Moeshart, Herman J. / 1987a
"Nederlanders en de invoering van de fotografie in Japan",*Herinneringen aan Japan 1850-1870 (yomigaeru Bakumatsu).* Prentenkabinet van de Rijksuniversiteit Leiden, ed. 's-Gravenhage: Staatsuitgeverij, pp.17-25.

1987b
Journaal van Jonkheer Dirk de Graeff van Polsbroek, 1857-1870. Belevenissen van een Nederlands diplomaat in het negentiende eeuwse Japan. Assen: van Gorcum.

Nihon shashinka kyōkai [Japan Photographers Association] (ed.) / 1971
Nihon shashinshi 1840-1945 [History of Japanese Photography, 1840-1945]. Tokyo: Heibonsha.

Ohara, Tetsuo (ed.) / 1983
Mōsu korekushon-shashinshū: hyakunen mae no Nihon [E.S. Morse Collection/Photography: Japan a Century Ago]. Tokyo: Shōgakukan.

Ono, Setsuko / 1972
A Western Image of Japan. What Did the West See Through the Eyes of Loti and Hearn?. Geneve: Imprimerie du Courrier.

Ozawa, Takeshi / 1981
"The History of Early Photography in Japan",*History of Photography,* vol.5, nr.4 (Oct.), pp. 285-303.

1986
Nihon no shashinshi
[History of Japanese Photography]. Tokyo: Nikkor Club.

1990
Shashin de miru Bakumatsu-Meiji [Bakumatsu and Meiji as Seen Through Photographs]. Tokyo: Sekaibunkasha.

Prentenkabinet van de Rijksuniversiteit

Leiden (ed.) / 1987
Herinneringen aan Japan, 1850-1870 (yomigaeru Bakumatsu). Foto's en fotoalbums in Nederlands bezit. 's-Gravenhage: Staatsuitgeverij.

Reischauer, Edwin O. / 1981
Japan: The Story of a Nation. New York: Alfred A. Knopf.

Robinson, Bonnell D. / 1988
"Transition and the Quest for Permanence: Photographers and Photographic Technology in Japan, 1854-1880s", *A Timely Encounter,* see Banta and Taylor, 1988, pp. 39-51.

Rosin, Henry / 1987
"Etudes sur les Débuts de la Photographie Japonaise au 19e Siècle", *Bulletin Association Franco-Japonaise,* no. 16 (Avril), pp. 33-9.

Saitō, Takio / 1987
"Yokohama shashin shōshi: F. Beato to Shimooka Renjō wo chushin ni" [A Short History of Yokohama Photography: The Circle of F. Beato and Shimooka Renjō], *F. Beato Bakumatsu Nihon shashinshū,* see Yokohama kaikō shiryōkan, 1987, pp. 169-198.

1990
"Yokohama shashin no sekai" [The World of Yokohama Photography] In: *Saishiki arubamu: Meiji no Nihon, `Yokohama shashin' no sekai,* see Yokohama kaikō shiryōkan, 1990, pp. 217-235.

Schaap, Robert (ed.) / 1987
Meiji, Japanese Art in Transition. Den Haag: Haags Gemeentemuseum.

Seidensticker, Edward / 1985
Low City, High City. Tokyo from Edo to the Earthquake, 1867-1923. Penguin Books edition.

Ukiyo-e Books / n.d. (1990)
Images of 19th Century Japan. Sale catalogue containing travelbooks, crepe books and photograph albums. Leiden: Ukiyo-e Books.

Waley, Paul / 1984
Tokyo Now and Then. An Explorer's Guide. New York and Tokyo: Weatherhill.

Worswick, Clark (ed.) / 1979
Japan. Photographs 1854-1905. New York: Pennwick Publishing Inc., and Alfred A. Knopf.

Yokohama kaikō shiryōkan [Reference Museum of Yokohama Freeport] (ed) / 1987
F. Beato Bakumatsu Nihon shashinshu [Collection of F. Beato's Photographs of Bakumatsu Japan]. Yokohama: Yokohama kaikō shiryō fukyū kyōkai.

1990
Saishiki arubamu: Meiji no Nihon, 'Yokohama shashin' no sekai [Coloured Albums: Meiji Japan, The World of 'Yokohama Photography']. Yokohama: Yūrindō.

Yokota, Yoichi / 1989
"Bakumatsu Meiji no shashinshi shoron" [A Short Treatise on the History of Photography in the Bakumatsu and Meiji Period], *Shashinshū: Meiji no Yokohama-Tokyo: nokosarete ita garasu kanban kara,* see Iwasaki Yoshiro ikueikai, 1989, pp. 171-181.

idem
"Shashin to kaiga" [Photography and Painting], pp. 186-93.

idem
"Shashinshi shōjiten" [Brief Dictionary of Photographers], pp. 1-16.